Linc

Heroic, Tragic & Bizarre

From History

Written by Mick Lake

Compiled and edited by Sue Lake

Copyright © Mick Lake 2023

All Rights Reserved

ISBN: 9798864088760

Dedication

This book is dedicated to the memory of our loving grandparents

Grace & Bert

Gladys & Harold

Winnie & Jack

Frances & Fred

Step-grandfather, Bill

Acknowledgements

This book could not have been produced without the help of numerous people who have offered their unstinting support and to whom I owe a huge debt of gratitude.

1) To Lee, Marilyn and Gina; Administrators of the Facebook group, *"You're probably from Lincoln if…"*, for allowing me to promote my books on your site.

2) To Zoe at "Duck Egg Blue" who has agreed to stock signed copies of my books in her delightful shop at 55, High Street, Saxilby, LN1 2HE.

3) To my long-suffering team of proof readers, Kyla, Mary and Sam, without whom my prose would be complete gibberish.

4) To Georgina Collingwood, Sharan Watkinson, Margaret Hewitt, and CF from Hoyland, for their invaluable contributions to the stories.

But above all, to my wife, Sue, who has kept me on the straight and narrow for 44 years. She has supported me tirelessly in all of my endeavours and has now assumed the role of researcher, compiler, proof reader and editor.

Thank you to each and every one of you from the bottom of my heart.

Introduction

"You have to know the past to understand the present"
Carl Sagan, (1980)

This book contains over 70 short stories, and closely follows the format of my first book, *Lincoln – True Tales from History*, which sold hundreds of copies across four continents. The first book had a strong focus upon extraordinarily tragic events, and this book contains many stories of a similar nature. However, this book also has many tales which demonstrate the selfless courage shown by ordinary people whilst going about their daily business.

The stories are all based in the city of Lincoln, or villages within the surrounding area, with the exception of a small number which describe the remarkable exploits of its citizens whilst travelling in other parts of the world.

Examples of the stories include:

- A man who escaped from Lincoln Castle (twice)
- Five Lincoln girls torpedoed in the Atlantic
- A woman who ran into a blazing house
- The couple who trafficked babies
- The woman who married her attacker
- Brave rescues in Lincoln's factories and waterways

If someone had told my younger self that I would spend my retirement writing about historical events, I would have responded with disbelief. History lessons at my secondary school in the late 1960s, were mainly about kings and queens who had been dead for centuries, and we had to learn the dates of various battles by rote. I could not see the point of it and dropped the subject at the earliest opportunity.

It was not until I started researching my own family history that I began to see how the things they tried to teach me at school had a direct impact on my very existence. I would not be here today if my great grandfather, Thomas, had not survived the Boer War and the military catastrophe at Gallipoli. The same is true in respect of my grandfather, Jack: when war was declared against Germany in 1939, he enlisted the very next day. It was only after he passed away, that I discovered he had been rescued from the sea at Dunkirk, took part in the D-Day landings, and formed part of the relief column at Arnhem.

However, it was events away from the battlefield which had an unexpected influence upon me, especially when I learned about the difficulties that some of my ancestors endured: I remember my great grandmother, Alice, as being a sweet old lady who once showed me how to skin a rabbit to prepare it for the pot. I now know that she was one of three illegitimate children, and that she was born in the workhouse where she endured untold hardships.

I never knew my grandfather, Fred, as he passed away when my mother was just five years old. He died from injuries that he received whilst working in a factory, leaving my young grandmother to raise four children without the benefit of the welfare state as we know it today. Before she passed away, my mother's older sister told me that the family were so poor in the 1930s that the five of them would share two boiled eggs for breakfast. She explained that her mother would remove the tops and bottoms of each egg, and share them between the two girls, whilst the two boys would each receive a middle section containing the yolk. When I asked my aunt the question, "What did grandma eat?" I was told, "She went hungry."

So, whilst I now have some understanding of how political and military events from the past shaped our current world, the thing that really resonates with me is how people going about their everyday lives coped with the life-changing events that impacted upon their families.

Every tale in this book is underpinned by meticulous research, and regardless of how bizarre it may seem, every story is completely true.

Donations to Good Causes

Sue and myself have pledged that we will donate all of the royalties from the sale of our books to good causes. To date, we have donated over £3,000. So, if you have previously purchased any of our books, thank you, and these are the good causes that you have helped:

- St Barnabas Lincolnshire (they provide end-of-life care within the patient's home, or in their hospice).

- Lincolnshire Integrated Voluntary Emergency Service, otherwise known as LIVES (their volunteers provide emergency medical care in critical situations).

- Blind Veterans UK, formerly known as St Dunstan's (They provide support to ex-servicemen and women to rebuild their lives after sight loss).

- Wildline Wildlife Sanctuary (specialises in rescuing tortoises, but also accepts badgers, bats, foxes, hedgehogs, squirrels, voles, and various breeds of birds).

- We have also donated to an appeal to support two children in Saxilby who have been diagnosed with a life-limiting genetic condition known as Metachromatic Leukodystrophy.

And finally…
Similar stories are published periodically on my Facebook Group "*Lincolnshire - True Tales from History*" which readers are welcome to join.

Contents

1	Thomas Gardiner	A Murdered Postboy
2	Peter Collins	Broke a Man's Skull
3	Paul Harding	An Exploding Canon
4	Elizabeth Sawyer	Humiliating Husband
5	Francis Ward	Cathedral Fire
6	Joseph Ralph	An Escape Artist
7	Ann Foster	A Spiteful Vicar
8	William Antcliffe	Thrashed with Nettles
9	Rebecca Sawyer	A Sordid Story
10	Elizabeth Pardon	Frightened to Death
11	Elizabeth Pickworth	Shot in the Kitchen
12	Welcome Fern	A Little Thief
13	George Seagrave	A Schoolboys' Duel
14	Rebecca Wheatley	Chained to a Wall
15	Henry Stebbings	Epic Police Pursuit
16	Dorothy Sparrow	Stabbed her Lover
17	Lewis Kirby	A Perverted Curate
18	Richard Atkinson	Reckless Curiosity
19	John Hickey	Fight for a Woman
20	Percy Blow	Heroic City Footballer
21	Anna Bell	Poisonous Medication
22	Maud Hunt	Burglar with a Bayonet
23	Eliza Luff	A Dying Declaration?
24	Walter Green	Rescued, but…
25	Dick Elderkin	Mauled by a Mad Dog
26	Nathan Bagley	Died for Love
27	Rose Dale	Senselessly Shot
28	Louisa North	A Forgiving Victim
29	Herbert Pickering	Drunken Wife-Beater
30	William Feary	A Mining Accident

31	Frank Clawson	An Abominable Man
32	Sarah Parrish	Sent for a Doctor
33	William Williamson	Tried his Best
34	Daisy Williams	A Sordid Case
35	Gertrude Makins	Beaten with a Poker
36	Martha Stothard	A Family Affair
37	Zilpah Cheseldine	A Painful Tragedy
38	Walter Reeve	A Runaway Horse
39	Rose Coles	A Dreadful Fall
40	George Meggitt	A Dangerous Game
41	James Upton	Conspicuous Gallantry
42	Linnell Family	Brothers in Arms
43	William Palmer	First Solo Flight
44	Mary Routledge	A Fatal Fire
45	Frederick Vickers	Rescued Two Men
46	George Baker	A Fit of Depression
47	Thomas Martin	A Faulty Rope
48	Ernest Rosling	A Fatal Miscalculation
49	George Dutton	Pram in the Fossdyke
50	Rhoda Carr	A Loaded Shotgun
51	Margaret Cordey	Coal Gas Tragedy
52	Ethel Garner	Strangled her Baby
53	Frank Jackson	A Furious Bull
54	Joseph Shelton	Accused of Theft
55	Arthur Lewin	A Plucky Gatekeeper
56	Robert Howden	A Bathing Bridegroom
57	David Shoebottom	A Brave Rescue
58	Gladys Field	Trafficked Babies
59	John Hill	A Bent Copper
60	Henry Twiggs	Liked Young Girls
61	Charles Oldham	A Tragic Coincidence

62	John Dixon	The George Cross
63	Sheila Caygill	An Evacuee
64	Lena Thacker	A Blazing House
65	Dorothy Fannen	Starved her Baby
66	Jack Kelway	A German Attack
67	Marjorie Griffen	Found in a Shed
68	Eileen Breeds	A Massive Bomb
69	Henry Tyler	A Million Pennies
70	Doris Ashby	Husband had Secrets!
71	Beryl Collingham	If I Don't Jump…
72	Evans Family	Air-Crash Fireball

1: Thomas Gardiner

Nettleham 1733: A Murdered Postboy

A headstone in the graveyard at All Saints Church, Nettleham, marks the final resting place of Thomas Gardiner. The inscription reads, *"Tho Gardiner post boy of Lincoln, barbarously murdered by Isaac & Tho Hallam, Jan 3 1733, aged 19."*

Thomas and Isaac Hallam were born in Leicestershire, in 1707 and 1709 respectively. The family subsequently relocated to Lincoln where Isaac obtained a job as a postboy when he was around 12 years old. His job required him to carry mail on horseback, or by horse-drawn cart, over long distances in all weathers. Isaac proved to be a conscientious and reliable employee but, when he was in his twenties, he started getting into financial difficulty as a result of heavy drinking and reckless gambling. Upon hearing of Isaac's problems, the postmaster (Mr Rands) offered to help, and kindly loaned him a considerable sum to clear his debts. However, Isaac continued to lead a dissipated lifestyle and he soon fell behind with his repayments. Mr Rands eventually lost his patience and had Isaac thrown into the debtor's prison. The date of his release has not been documented, but some accounts (e.g. Wynn, 2012), suggest that Mr Rands had taken pity upon him and revoked the debt.

After his release, Isaac teamed up with Thomas and the two brothers embarked on a protracted crime spree. They operated as highwaymen on foot, or on horseback, across a wide swathe of countryside between Lincoln and London. Typically, their victims would be travelling alone, and they were ambushed on deserted country lanes.

On January 2nd, 1733, a postboy named William Wright was travelling to Market Rasen when he was ambushed near Faldingworth. The assailants rifled his pockets, stole the two horses, and cut the lad's throat. His body was found the next morning.

The following day, Thomas Gardiner was travelling from Lincoln to Langworth with a bag of mail. He never reached his destination. His body, and that of his horse, were found with their throats cut at Bunker's Hill on the outskirts of Lincoln. Some writers (e.g. Major, 2016), claim that Thomas, "Was forced to blow his horn, before his tormentors told him that he had just sounded his own death peal."

Suspicion fell upon two dubious characters who had been seen in the area, and a reward of £40 (worth around £12,000 in today's money) was offered for their capture. A very detailed description of the men was published as follows. "One of the persons supposed to have committed the said murder is a slender bodied man with a thin face, wearing a light coloured wig, and a white straight-bodied coat, with carved buttons on it, along with a blue riding-coat, lined with yellow, and with brass buttons." His accomplice was described as, "Pale-faced and marked with the small pox; he had on a straight bodied grey double-breasted coat with black buttons, and a light-coloured riding coat."

The two men evaded capture for a few weeks but their luck ran out when they were arrested for a completely different matter in Wiltshire. A warden at Salisbury Gaol recognised the two men from their description and claimed the reward. Isaac and Thomas Hallam were conveyed to Lincoln by carriage on a journey which took several days. News of their imminent arrival had spread throughout the city, and crowds started to gather at Bar Gate and along the route to the castle. The brothers were then greeted with hisses, boos and jeers from the crowd, along with loud blasts on their horns by a group of postboys.

The brothers appeared before Mr Justice Probyn at the Lent Assizes. They were convicted of the murders of William Wright and Thomas Gardiner, and condemned to die. Before the sentence was carried out, Isaac revealed that he had targeted the two postboys as a way of exacting his revenge on Mr Rands. He then confessed that, along with Thomas, he had committed a total of 63 robberies and another murder.

At 9am on March 20th, 1733, the brothers were taken from Lincoln Castle to Bunker's Hill, where gallows had been erected at the spot where Thomas Gardiner had been murdered. Thomas Hallam was forced to watch as his brother was placed in irons and hung by his neck until he was dead. Thomas Hallam was then taken 8 miles further to Faldingworth Gate, to the spot where William Wright had been murdered. He was then placed in irons and hung.

What happened next?

The Judge specified that, after being hung, Isaac and Thomas Hallam should be gibbetted. Their bodies were covered in tar and suspended in iron cages at the places where they committed their crimes as a warning to others. A gibbet would often remain in place for many years until nothing more than a skeleton remained.

Thomas was buried on January 6th, 1733. His grave, and its headstone, can still be found in the churchyard at Nettleham.

According to Major (2016), William Wright was buried in Market Rasen, but the author was unable to find a corresponding entry in the parish records.

Primary sources:

Stamford Mercury, March 22nd, 1733
Ipswich Journal, March 10th, 1733
Wynn, D., Lincolnshire Villains: Rogues, Rascals and Reprobates, (The History Press, 2012)
Major, J., Grisly Murder in Eighteenth Century Lincolnshire, (Wordpress, 2016)

Research notes:

It is common knowledge that, in the UK, a new year starts on January 1st. However, this was not always the case and in the early 1700's, the church celebrated new year on March 25th to coincide with Annunciation Day. Consequently, Thomas's baptism is recorded as February 19th 1713/14, and his burial took place on January 6th 1732/33.

The author's research identified a report in the Stamford Mercury dated March 22nd, 1733, which states that the brothers were executed on "Friday last". Therefore, to avoid confusion, the author has chosen to express the year as 1733 throughout this story.

2: Peter Collins

Branston - 1838: Broke a Man's Skull

Peter Collins was born in County Mayo, Ireland, in 1818. The family lived, and worked, on the Clanmorris Estate owned by Lord Oranmore. When he was in his late teens, Collins emigrated to England and became part of a team of Irish agricultural labourers in Lincolnshire.

At 10am on Tuesday, September 4th, 1838, Collins was with seven other men who went into the Plough Public House, Branston, where they consumed a considerable quantity of ale. Around 12 noon, the group were joined by a 48-year-old Irishman named Michael Nestor (sometimes given as Nester) and three other men. The group of 12 men enjoyed a hearty meal of bacon and ordered more ale.

When Nestor paid for his drink, he handed over a sovereign. The coin had a face value of £1, and would be worth around £140 in today's money. Nestor received 19 shillings and 7 pence in change and placed the money in his waistcoat pocket. Collins and Nestor then made their way to the Wagon and Horses where they both consumed another glass of ale.

They left the Wagon and Horses around 1pm, and staggered through the village in the general direction of Lincoln. Shortly after passing Branston Park, the two men went through a gate, crossed a yard, and entered a dilapidated building which had formerly been used as a bakehouse. At this point, Collins grabbed a hoe and hit Nestor's head so hard, that the shaft of the tool broke in two. Collins then picked up a heavy stick and beat Nestor with it repeatedly until he lost consciousness. He then took the money from Nestor's waistcoat pocket and started walking away rather quickly.

A woman who lived nearby had been alerted by the commotion and witnessed the latter part of the attack. She screamed loudly, and neighbours apprehended Collins. Upon being searched, the stolen money was found in his possession. Michael Nestor received medical attention for a fractured skull, and lingered for two days before passing away. Collins was charged with murder and remanded in custody.

Michael Collins appeared before Mr Justice Bosenquet at the Lincolnshire Assizes, on March 9th, 1839, charged with having murdered Michael Nestor. The court heard compelling evidence which showed, beyond all reasonable doubt, that Collins had inflicted the injuries. In his defence, Collins said that Nestor had started quarrelling with him and that Nestor had struck the first blow.

At this point the court heard from Lord Oranmore who had travelled up from London that morning. He testified that he knew Peter Collins very well and that he was, "A man of good character and peaceable conduct." The Jury found Collins Not Guilty of murder, but Guilty of manslaughter. Peter Collins was sentenced to be, "Transported beyond the seas for the remainder of his life".

What happened next?

Michael Nestor was buried at All Saints Church, Branston, on September 6th, 1838. He was 48 years old and had never married.

On July 27th, 1839, Collins was transported from Lincoln Gaol to the prison hulk Ganymede, which was moored in the Thames Estuary. He remained there until October 10th, 1839, when he was one of 230 convicts who were transferred to a ship named the Woodbridge. The vessel arrived in New South Wales, Australia, on February 27th, 1840, and he was set to work in the Moreton Bay district.

Australian convict records show that Peter Collins was subsequently granted a "ticket of leave" where he was permitted to leave prison with certain restrictions placed upon him. Records of his life beyond this point are inconclusive.

Primary source; Nottingham and Newark Mercury, September 15th, 1838

3: Paul Harding

Lincoln - 1846: An Exploding Cannon

Details of Paul Harding's early life are a bit sketchy, but he was born around 1786 and it is probable that he was originally from Tetbury in Gloucestershire. As a young man he joined an Artillery Regiment of the British Army. He served throughout the Peninsula War (1807-1814) in Spain and Portugal, and was also at the Battle of Waterloo in 1815 (see footnote). He emerged without a scratch, and settled down in Lincoln after he left the army.

On Monday, August 2nd, 1846, Paul was participating in festivities to celebrate the grand opening of the Nottingham to Lincoln railway line. The new station (later known as St Mark's Station) was festooned with bunting, a band played music, and the cathedral bells were peeling for most of the day. To add some panache, Paul was asked to "announce" the arrival and departure of every train by firing a cannon in the shunting yard.

The sound of the cannon boomed across the city all day during which over 10,000 people visited the station to witness the spectacle. Then, as the last excursion train of the day approached the station, Paul prepared the cannon for its final shot. He rammed powder down the muzzle followed by damp sand, just as he had been doing all day. As the train slowed at the platform, Paul ignited the fuse.

This time however, the cannon exploded and sent splinters of shrapnel across the immediate area. Paul's leg received dreadful wounds and two other men received less serious injuries. Paul was given first aid at the scene and taken to hospital where surgeons had to amputate one of his legs.

Paul never recovered from his injuries and passed away on Monday, August 17th, 1846. At his inquest it was claimed that

Paul had been a heavy drinker for several years and was under the influence of alcohol whilst firing the cannon. The cannon was described as being old and rusty. The jury returned a verdict of "Accidental death."

Paul Harding was a single man, and was thought to have been about 60 years old. He was buried in St Swithin's Cemetery on August 20th, 1846.

Primary Source: Sheffield Independent, August 8th, 1846.

Research note:

The Waterloo Medal is a military decoration which was conferred upon every soldier (officer or otherwise) who fought at the Battle of Waterloo in 1815. Records show that the medal was awarded to Paul Harding and that he was a member of D Troop of the Corps of Royal Artillery Drivers.

4: Elizabeth Sawyer

Nettleham - 1851: A Humiliating Husband

Elizabeth was born at Ruskington (near Sleaford) in 1819 to Thomas and Mary Claricoates. Records from All Saints Church in the village show that she had six siblings who were born between 1817 and 1832. She married William Thomas Matthews at Newark in 1842 and their two children, Mary and Ann, were both born in Nettleham before 1847. Tragically, William passed away in August 1849, leaving Elizabeth in a precarious situation. After a brief period of mourning, she set about finding a new husband.

Samuel Sawyer was an agricultural labourer who had been born and raised in Nettleham. He was widely regarded as being "a brute" but he promised to take care of Elizabeth and her two children. The couple were married at All Saints Church in Nettleham on April 1st, 1850, but their marital bliss was short-lived.

Eighteen months later, on Friday, October 24th, 1851, Samuel pulled heavily pregnant Elizabeth from her bed and subjected her to a humiliating and degrading experience. Firstly, he made her wear a horse's halter. He then attached a lead and, by using threats against her, dragged her down to the White Hart beer house in the village. She was wearing nothing but her night clothes. A local farmer named Proctor then acted as "auctioneer" to sell Elizabeth to the highest bidder. The first bid was for half a yard of ale. A blacksmith, named Jubb, offered 5 shillings. A miller, named Pearson, offered another 5 shillings if he could make up a "threesome". The clerk of the parish council, Richard Johnson, then increased the bid to a sovereign (20 shillings). Samuel announced he wanted 30 shillings for the pleasure of his wife and when that sum was not forthcoming, he withdrew the "lot" and took her back home. Samuel was not prosecuted for this incident but the Lincolnshire Chronicle published an article which described a "most disgusting exhibition" and as a consequence his employer, Mr Bayles, sacked him.

Elizabeth gave birth to a healthy baby boy 14 days later.

What happened next?

Elizabeth must have wondered what the future held for her but she decided to stay with Samuel and she gave him three more children over the following decade.

There were no further reports of Samuel being unkind to Elizabeth but he was in trouble with the law on numerous occasions, including:
- He was fined 5 shillings in 1860 for "cruelly beating" a five-year-old boy from the village.
- In 1865 he was prosecuted in respect of an incident involving his own daughter (see chapter 9).
- He was found Guilty of ill-treating a horse in 1871 and was fined 18 shillings.
- In 1880 he deliberately drove his carriage at a group of children who were playing on Nettleham village green. He ran over a four-year-old girl and broke her thigh bone. He was sued for damages and had to pay £15.

Despite the obvious flaws in Samuel's character, Elizabeth stood by him for the remainder of her life. She died from natural causes in 1889, aged 70, and was laid to rest in the graveyard at Nettleham Church.

Samuel Sawyer died in 1898, aged 76 years, and shares a grave with Elizabeth.

Primary source: Lincolnshire Chronicle, October 31st, 1851

5: Francis Ward

Lincoln - 1853: The Cathedral Fire

Francis was born in Chelmsford (Essex) on June 25th, 1820. He was one of six children whose parents were John (a clergyman) and Amelia Ward. In 1837 he entered Woolwich Military Academy as an officer cadet and was commissioned as a 2nd Lieutenant in 1839. By 1848 he had been promoted to Captain and was assigned as the commanding officer of the artillery company at "The Drop Redoubt" in Dover.

Meanwhile in 1845, his father had been appointed as Dean of Lincoln Cathedral. Captain Ward was a regular visitor to the city and soon got to know the cathedral and its staff. One such visit took place during February 1853, when he happened to be in the right place, at the right time.

Wednesday, February 23rd, 1853 started as a bitterly cold day but, by mid-afternoon, the city was bathed in bright sunshine. However. at 3:30pm, the wind which had been blowing steadily from the west, suddenly veered to due north and "Its intensity increased to that of a perfect hurricane. The sky became overcast and there commenced a blinding snow storm." Then at 4pm, the city reverberated to the tumultuous sound of a clap of thunder and a bolt of lightning streaked across the sky towards the cathedral. Shortly after 6pm, a man rushed into the cathedral and reported that he could see flames oozing from the north west pinnacle of the central tower. Mr Clark, the verger, was immediately informed and he instructed the fire bell should be rung. Some 60 men from the surrounding area, including Captain Ward, rushed to help.

At this point, Captain Ward's leadership skills became evident and he organised the men into an effective firefighting team. After scaling 338 steps to climb the tower, he saw that flames were leaping some 3-4 feet into the air, from an area of smouldering woodwork at the base of the pinnacle. The volunteers formed a human chain to convey water from two large water tanks within the tower. At the same time a builder, named Kirk, used a spade as an improvised axe to chop away the burning embers and sparks flew away on the howling wind. The blaze was quickly brought under control, and wet blankets were draped over the affected area. As a precautionary measure, Captain Ward then assigned men to stand by with buckets of water in case of another outbreak.

The Cathedral had been saved from extensive damage and a valuable lesson had been learned. The Dean and Chapter heard that it would cost less than £10 to repair the damage, and they accepted an architect's recommendation to protect the building with lightening conductors. As a gesture of gratitude each of the 60 men who helped fight the fire was rewarded with a gift of 3 shillings.

What happened to Captain Ward?

In 1855 he was sent to Crimea. He commanded a troop of the Royal Horse Artillery at the Battle of Tchernaya and served at the Siege of Sevastopol. Whilst in Crimea, he became very concerned about the unsanitary conditions that the army endured and wrote to Lord Palmerston indicating that 20-30 men were dying every day due to cholera. In another letter Francis spoke of meeting Florence Nightingale. He survived the conflict and was promoted to Major upon his return to England.

He married Emily Bridgeman in Shropshire in 1859. The couple made their home in Woolwich and subsequently had 5 children. By the time he retired in 1864, he held the rank of Lieutenant Colonel. It seems however, that the horrors of war had an adverse effect upon his mental health and he was admitted to Manor House Lunatic Asylum in July, 1871. He remained there until he died on January 12th 1876, aged 56.

Primary Source: Lincolnshire Chronicle, March 4th, 1853

Research note:

Some contemporary newspaper accounts of this incident refer to the cathedral having been struck by a meteor. However, the report presented to the Dean and Chapter, identified that lightning struck the top of the pinnacle and the electrical charge then tracked downwards, melting some of the lead during its journey. It was suggested that woodwork, which was scorched by the electrical charge, was fanned by the strong wind for two hours before the flames became visible.

6: Joseph Ralph

Lincoln - 1855: An Escape Artist

Details of Joseph's early life have not been clearly documented, but most accounts claim he was born in 1819, and was kidnapped from his parents in York by a sophisticated criminal gang when he was just six years old. In the first instance, he was shown how to climb through small windows so that he could open locks from the inside, or pass stolen goods out through the window to his accomplices. As he grew older he was taught how to use a wide variety of housebreaking implements and how to pick locks.

The first conviction recorded against Joseph Ralph in Lincolnshire was on July 26th, 1854, when he was charged with one count of burglary at a bank in Grimsby, and two more at Barton and Barrow, during which he stole several items of silverware from dwelling houses. The court found him Guilty. However, before sentence was passed, the Judge heard evidence from the governor of the Kirton House of Correction. The governor testified that he recognised the defendant as being the same person who, under the name of Thomas Thompson, had been convicted of a felony in 1846 and sentenced to seven years transportation. Mr Justice Maule then sentenced Joseph to 20 years transportation and he was placed in a cell at Lincoln Castle until the arrangements could be made for him to be transferred to London.

On Friday, July 28th, Joseph was visited in his cell by the Reverend Holden who urged him to reform. When the priest left, the cell door was inadvertently left unlocked and Joseph saw an opportunity to escape. He used old blankets, a stool and a handkerchief to fashion a primitive "dummy" and placed it on his bed to make it appear that he was fast asleep. Meanwhile, he slipped out of the cell, closed the cell door behind him, and hid in a closet until nightfall. After the warders had done their final rounds, he gained access to the prison garden, then scaled two large stone walls to secure his freedom. When his absence was discovered at 5am the following morning, an extensive search was made of the immediate area and his description was conveyed by telegraph to other parts of the county.

On Monday, July 31st, Joseph was seen loitering on the banks of the Humber, near Barton, by Constables Clayton and Jubb who were accompanied by a man named Godfrey. When the officers seized Joseph, he put up a struggle and all four men ended up on the ground. At this point Joseph produced a clasp knife. He gave Godfrey a deep cut to his thigh and slashed Constable Jubb across his wrist. Constable Clayton however was a powerfully-built man who skilfully disarmed Joseph and completely subdued him. Joseph was then taken to the police lock-up in Barton, where he glibly boasted that since his escape from the castle he had burgled houses in Torksey, Gainsborough and Barton. The following day, Joseph was bound with ropes and returned to Lincoln Castle. Upon his arrival, he was shackled with a set of leg-irons which were connected by a chain to a manacle on his left wrist. Joseph was then placed in a cell on the first floor under close guard, but he was already plotting his next escape.

His heavy cell door had a single lock on the outer side of the door and a small hatch which warders would use to pass food and drink to prisoners. There were two keys to the lock; one was carried by the warders, the other by the chaplain. Over the course of the next few weeks the chaplain paid several visits to Joseph and, on one occasion, he placed the cell key on a small table in full view. This was the opportunity that Joseph had been waiting for. He discretely studied the key, memorised its size and shape, and made a sketch of it as soon as the chaplain departed. Over the following weeks he used stale bread to made a mould. He then used heat from the lantern in his cell to melt his pewter mug, and poured the molten metal into the improvised mould.

On the night of Monday, October 2nd, 1854, Joseph somehow managed to open the small hatch in his cell door. Then, by pushing his arm and shoulder though the aperture, he could just reach the lock and he opened it using the key that he had fashioned. He used rags to stifle the sound of his shackles clanking together and tip-toed along the central gallery to a kitchen where he stole a coat. He then passed through some iron gates, and reached the castle yard where he found a ladder which enabled him to scale the castle walls. Joseph then used his lock-picking skills to remove his shackles and made a clean getaway from the city.

By the early hours of Thursday, October 5th, Joseph had made his way to Nottingham. As he crossed over the Trent Bridge, he was challenged by Constable Bostock who demanded to know what he was up to. Joseph did not reply, but immediately struck the officer's head with a heavy stick. Bostock's hat was broken by the force of the blow but he shouted for help and started grappling with Joseph. It seemed that Joseph was getting the upper hand, before a man named Birkin came to the officer's assistance and helped to place Joseph in handcuffs. Joseph was taken to a nearby police station and, when searched, it was found that he was in possession of housebreaking implements and the pewter key which he had used to affect his escape.

Joseph was returned to Lincoln Castle where he was placed in two sets of leg-irons, manacles on both wrists, and a set of heavy chains linking his feet to his arms in a way which severely restricted his movement. Two warders were then placed outside his cell to keep him under constant vigilance. Joseph remained there until March 8th, 1855, when he was brought before the court charged with the knife attack on Constable Jubb and with being unlawfully at large. He was sentenced to 18 months imprisonment on the first charge, and transportation for life in connection with his escapes.

On January 3rd, 1856, Joseph Ralph left the shores of his native land for the last time. He was one of 250 convicts aboard the William Hammond, which arrived at Fremantle, Western Australia, on March 29th. He was incarcerated in Fremantle prison and was initially given work in the prison library. He was not however, a model prisoner. Records show that on August

18th, 1857, he received 75 strokes of the cat o' nine tails for attempting to escape through a gate in the perimeter wall.

This punishment did not dampen Joseph's enthusiasm for freedom and, by 1864, he had made six further attempts to escape which resulted in him being placed in solitary confinement. Over the next ten years, Joseph made four more attempts to escape from his solitary cell. Finally, in 1874, the Comptroller-General ordered that Joseph's cell should be reinforced with gratings fixed to the windows, and that iron plating (secured with headless screws) should be fastened to all other parts of his cell. Prison guards were then placed in empty cells either side and directly beneath Joseph's cell, with orders that he was to be strip searched twice each day.

Joseph did not attempt to escape again and died in the prison hospital at Freemantle, in 1887. He was approximately 68 years old.

Primary sources:
Lincolnshire Chronicle, July 28th 1854
Hull Advertiser, August 5th, 1854
Nottingham Journal, October 6th, 1854
www.convictrecords.com.au
www.freemantleprison.com.au

Research notes:

Records relating to a prisoner named Thomas Thompson being convicted at Kirton Lindsey and being transported for seven years could not been found. However, in July 1846, a man using the name Thomas Johnson was convicted at Kirton in Lindsey for a felony in Gainsborough and sentenced to 10 years transportation. The man attempted to escape from custody whilst at Kirton and was then swiftly transferred to Millbank Penitentiary in London. There is however, no record of a man with these details boarding a ship and arriving in Australia, so it's likely that the man either died in prison or escaped from custody.

7: Ann Foster

Stow - 1858: A Spiteful Vicar

Records from St Chad's Church, Dunholme, show that Ann was baptised on March 3rd, 1822, and was one of six children born to Joseph (a labourer) and Ann Foster. The 1841 census shows that she was then a domestic servant at Aswarby Hall (near Sleaford).

On October 17th, 1842, Ann married a stonemason, called Joseph Newton, at St Andrew's Church, Kirton in Lindsey. Ann became pregnant the following year and their daughter, Emma, was baptised at Dunholme on October 3rd, 1843.

The nature of Joseph Newton's work often took him away from home for protracted periods of time, so there was nothing unusual when he gathered his tools and left home to start a new job during the summer of 1845. Uncharacteristically however, Joseph did not send word about where he was going, or when he would return. Then, as the days turned into weeks, and the weeks turned into months, it slowly dawned upon Ann that Joseph was probably not coming back.

In desperation, she turned to her widowed father who was, by now, living in the small village of Stow near Gainsborough. Joseph Foster allowed Ann and Emma to move into his cottage and, in return, Ann cooked and kept house for her father. This arrangement continued for almost 11 years during which time she had heard nothing from Joseph Newton. She eventually concluded that he must be dead.

Ann, still only 34 years old, formed a relationship with a local man named George Credland, and moved in with him sometime during 1856. Ann became pregnant the following year and gave birth to a baby daughter who was baptised as Sarah Ann Credland, at St Mary's Church, Stow, on the 19th of July 1858. Sadly, shortly after Sarah was baptised, Ann became seriously ill with dropsy (now known as oedema). A doctor was summoned but, despite his best efforts, Ann's condition continued to deteriorate.

The Reverend George Atkinson was the incumbent at St Mary's Church in Stow, and came to visit Ann as she lay on her death bed. But, rather than providing emotional and spiritual support in her hour of need, he did quite the opposite. He announced that, as Ann had no proof that her first husband was dead, she was in an adulterous relationship. He went on to explain that, if she died "in that state", then she could not receive forgiveness from God, and could not go to heaven. Her only option, he insisted, was to leave George and return to live under her father's roof. Ann flatly refused, and the vicar went away with his tail between his legs.

The Reverend Atkinson returned to the house a few days later, but George Credland's mother refused to open the door to him. The clergyman was however, determined to confront Ann, and he barged his way into the cottage. He then went straight to Ann's bedside and informed her that, if she was not prepared to return to her father's house, he would refuse to give her a Christian burial. Ann lingered for a few more days, but passed away the following Saturday.

Ann's funeral took place on Monday afternoon. A grave had been prepared in the churchyard, but the Reverend Atkinson stuck to his guns; he refused to allow her remains to enter the church, and he would not allow the bell to be tolled. Ann's body was lowered into the ground in silence and the family were not permitted to erect a headstone.

What happened next?

The Reverend Atkinson was roundly condemned for his actions in newspapers across England. However, he was allowed to remain in post until his death in 1865. He is now widely remembered for being, "A single-minded bulldozer of a man" in respect of his Herculean efforts to restore the (then) dilapidated church building.

Tragically Ann's daughter, Sarah, passed away when she was just 6 months old. Parish records show that she was buried in St Mary's Churchyard, Stow, on January 26th, 1859.

Records relating to Emma are inconclusive.

Primary Sources;
Leeds Times, August 28th, 1858
Sturton and Stow History Society (online)

Research notes:

Newspaper reports at the time suggested that Sarah Newton and George Credland were married, but Sarah Ann Credland's baptism records show her mother's name as being Ann Newton rather than Ann Credland as one would expect if the couple were married.

8: William Antcliffe

South Carlton - 1864: Thrashed with Nettles

William was born at Stanton, Derbyshire, in 1843 to William (a bricklayer) and Mary Antcliffe. He was the eldest of three children. By 1851 the family had moved to Gringley on the Hill and lived at Lock Cottage, next to the Chesterfield Canal. After leaving school William served an apprenticeship as a builder for Jabez Taylor in nearby Gainsborough. On April 13th, 1864, William joined Lincolnshire Constabulary. He underwent a short period of basic training before being posted to the village of South Carlton (three miles north of Lincoln), on the last day of May. He took lodgings with the Vickers family, in a cottage on the outskirts of the village.

On Thursday, July 14th, 1864, Mrs Ann Vickers prepared breakfast for William which he ate heartily. He then donned his uniform and left the house shortly before 9am. He informed Mrs Vickers that he would return around 1:15pm. However, he did not return until 3:15pm, but gave no explanation as to why he was late. His lunch was set on the table, but he did not touch it. He then sat himself down in a chair, holding his head in his hands. He complained of having toothache and asked whether Mrs Vickers had any laudanum for the pain. Mrs Vickers poured a few drops of laudanum onto a piece of lint and suggested that William should place it against his gums. She returned the bottle to the cupboard and went out to the vegetable plot in her garden.

About 10 minutes later, Mrs Vickers' young son came up to her and said, "The policeman is making some strange noises." Mrs Vickers went back into the house and found that William had locked himself in the room. She demanded that he should open it, but the officer simply replied, "Goodbye. I have poisoned myself." Mrs Vickers then went outside and looked through the window into the room. She saw that the bottle of laudanum was now on the table. She sent for her neighbour, Mrs Westerfield, and the two women managed to break the door open. William pointed to the bottle and said, "I've drunk the lot." Mrs Westerfield asked, "Oh, what have you done that for?" William, who seemed to the in great agony, replied, "I will not declare the reason to any person. I'll go to hell first." They sent for a doctor and asked that he should come urgently.

Mrs Westerfield prepared a mixture of salt, water, and mustard in an attempt to make William vomit, but he would not drink it. William then gave £2 to Mrs Vickers saying, "This is for my board and lodgings, I will not die in debt." The two women helped William get to his feet and started walking him around the room, in an attempt to ensure he remained conscious until the doctor arrived. Around 3:45pm, William was no longer able to stand, even with assistance, and he slumped into a chair. He was still conscious, and started speaking of having been a sinner all of his life, and that he deserved to be punished. He went on to say that he had been feeling that way for 14 months and thanked Mrs Vickers for her kindness. William lost consciousness at 4pm.

Doctor Broadbent arrived from Lincoln at 5:45pm. He used a stomach pump to extract the contents of William's stomach and then thrashed William with stinging nettles (see footnote), without success. William was then taken to hospital in Lincoln by cart, where a powerful galvanic battery (see footnote) was connected to his chest in an attempt to stimulate muscular movement. Sadly, the best medical treatment available at the time was completely ineffective, and William passed away shortly after 7pm.

A Coroner's Inquest was held at the Black Boy public house, Lincoln, the following day. The Jury heard that William had a sweetheart, known only as Miss Ward. William and Miss Ward had been writing letters to each other on a very regular basis. William received a letter from her the day before he took his own life and destroyed it immediately after he read it. There was some speculation that William's claim to have toothache might have been a ploy on his part to obtain laudanum. After careful consideration, the Jury returned a verdict that the deceased had,

"Destroyed himself by taking the poison, but there was insufficient evidence as to the state of his mind at the time."

Constable William Antcliffe was 21 years old, and was laid to rest in plot A2172 at Canwick Road Old Cemetery, Lincoln.

Primary source: Nottinghamshire Guardian, July 22nd 1864

Footnotes: The practice of "urtication", or the thrashing a patient with stinging nettles, was traditionally used as a last resort, in the treatment of conditions such as palsy or paralysis. In the present day, some practitioners of herbal medicine recommend the procedure as a treatment for certain forms of arthritis.

In 1780, an Italian physician called Luigi Galvani, discovered that a spark from an electrical generator could produce twitching movements in the muscles of dead frogs, and he theorised that the phenomenon could have widespread medical uses. The process of Galvanism was brought to the attention of the general public in 1831 when Mary Shelly published her book, Frankenstein, and a highly sophisticated form of Galvanism is used in present day defibrillators.

9: Rebecca Sawyer

Nettleham - 1865: A Sordid Story

Rebecca was born at Nettleham, in 1854, to Samuel (an agricultural labourer) and Elizabeth Sawyer. She was one of six children in the house, but the eldest two girls were from their mother's previous marriage (see Chapter 4).

On April 28th, 1865, Rebecca's father had spent the afternoon in Lincoln, and he had been drinking. When he came home he asked Rebecca, then aged 11, to come into the parlour with him but she refused. He chased her and dragged her back to the parlour, where he threw her onto the bed and started molesting her.

Rebecca's younger brother William (aged 10) had found the house door was locked from the inside, so he went to the parlour window and watched his father on the bed with Rebecca. Samuel angrily sent William away to water his horse, which the boy did. William returned several minutes later and saw his father was still on the bed with Rebecca. Samuel told the boy he must go and watch for his mother returning home. William dutifully did as he was told and, when he saw her cart approaching, he ran back to the window to tell his father. Samuel told Rebecca that he would kill her if she said anything to her mother.

Later that evening Rebecca fled from her home to seek refuge with a near-neighbour, Samuel Kirk. Rebecca was in tears and "her hair was all-down". She told Mr Kirk what had happened and the police were informed. Samuel was arrested the following day and charged with attempting to rape Rebecca or, alternatively, with indecently assaulting her.

Samuel appeared at the Lindsey Quarter Sessions on June 30th, 1865. He was represented by Mr Yeatman QC and pleaded Not Guilty. Evidence was given by Rebecca about what her father had done to her. William and Mr Kirk then testified about what they had seen and heard. At this point, Mr Yeatman argued that the case rested on the uncorroborated evidence of two children and that it was not safe to convict. The Jury retired and, after due deliberation, returned a verdict of "Not Guilty on the first charge, but Guilty on the second charge of indecently assaulting Rebecca." Samuel was sentenced to two years imprisonment with hard labour.

The 1871 census shows that after his release, and somewhat surprisingly by today's standards, Samuel had returned to the matrimonial home and continued to live under the same roof as Rebecca.

What happened next?

In 1873, Rebecca married Thomas Bows, who was the licensee of the Black Horse Inn at Nettleham. The couple had seven children. Rebecca was widowed in 1906 but continued to run the Black Horse until her own death in 1915, aged 60 years. She was buried in Nettleham churchyard along with her husband.

Rebecca's brother, William, married Louise Marrows in 1883 and over the next 25 years they had 22 children. He died in 1935, aged 79.

Primary source: Lincolnshire Chronicle, July 7th, 1865

10: Elizabeth Pardon

Lincoln - 1866: Frightened to death

Elizabeth was born in Lincoln on the 23rd of January, 1859, to James (a boiler maker) and Ann Pardon (sometimes given as Parton). The 1861 census shows that she was the eldest of two children and that the family lived at 5, Industry Place (off Norman Street), in Lincoln. Church records show that she was baptised at St Swithin's Church on the 3rd of August 1863, but no other details of her young life have been recorded.

Admission records for Lincoln Union Workhouse for the period 1843-1871 have not survived but we know that by the Spring of 1866, Elizabeth had been admitted and shared a bed with a 10-year-old girl named Margaret Roberts.

On Sunday, 18th of March, 1866, Margaret got out of bed around 7:00am to answer a call of nature. When she returned, she noticed that Elizabeth was still asleep. Margaret then wrapped herself in a white sheet, pretending to be a ghost, and awakened Elizabeth from her slumber. Elizabeth was startled by the frightening vision before her eyes and started convulsing. Staff were alerted and they sent for Doctor Broadbent. Sadly, Elizabeth did not respond to treatment, and she passed away later that morning.

A Coroner's Inquest was held at the workhouse on Wednesday, April 4th, where Margaret admitted having tried to frighten Elizabeth for "a bit of fun". After hearing medical evidence from Doctor Broadbent, the Coroner's Jury returned the verdict that Elizabeth had, "Died from fright."

It is thought that Elizabeth, aged seven, was buried in an unmarked grave.

What happened next?

The 1871 census shows that Margaret Roberts had left the workhouse and had become a domestic servant for Henry Atterby (station master) at Harmston. She married Christopher Broadley in 1873 and the couple had a son (also named Christopher) in 1884.

Margaret tragically died from natural causes in 1888, aged 33 years.

Primary source: Stamford Mercury, April 6th, 1866

11: Elizabeth Pickworth

Doddington - 1868: Shot in the Kitchen

Elizabeth was born at East Markham, Nottinghamshire, in 1814, to Francis and Priscilla Jackson. She went into service as a teenager, and married Francis Whitaker at East Retford in 1840. Tragically, her husband passed away the following year. Elizabeth continued working as a domestic servant for various employers and eventually found herself in the small village of Doddington, some six miles west of Lincoln.

Benjamin Pickworth lived at Pigot Farm, on the outskirts of the village, and farmed 101 acres of land. His wife Betsey had passed away in 1847 and his elderly mother had helped him to raise their five children. Elizabeth and Benjamin were suited to one another and married at St Peter's Church, Doddington, on June 12th, 1854. She moved into the farmhouse and was "Loved dearly' by all of her step-children.

On Monday, June 15th, 1868, Elizabeth was sat on a chair in the kitchen surrounded by other members of the household. Around 9:30am, her step-son Joseph (aged 22) walked into the room. He removed a double-barrelled shotgun from the cupboard, where it was normally kept, and put it over his left arm. He then went to a drawer and took out a powder flask, a shot flask, and some wads. At that moment the gun went off, and Elizabeth fell lifeless from her chair with grievous injuries to the left side of her head. Joseph galloped to Saxilby on his horse and returned with Doctor Rainbird. Sadly, life was extinct and there was nothing he could do.

An Inquest was held at the farm the following morning where a servant, named Mary Law, said she had been sewing in the kitchen at the time of the tragedy and it seemed that the gun had just gone off on its own. The Coroner's Jury also heard from Benjamin Pickworth (aged 28) who said that on the morning of

Sunday, June 14th, he had taken the shotgun out of the cupboard and loaded it with the intention of shooting sparrows. However, when a servant informed him that the rest of the family were just coming back from church, he put the shotgun back into the cupboard. Joseph Pickworth then testified that he had last used the shotgun on Saturday, June 13th, and it was unloaded when he returned it to the cupboard. He assumed it was still unloaded when he removed it from the cupboard on Monday and thought it likely that his watch chain had caught the right-hand lock, causing the gun to go off. The Jury returned a unanimous verdict of "Accidental death."

Elizabeth was laid to rest at St Peter's Church in Doddington on June 17th, 1868. She was 55 years old.

Primary source: Lincolnshire Chronicle, June 19th, 1868

12: Welcome Fern

Lincoln - 1868: A Little Thief

Welcome was born in Lincoln in 1861 to James (a fishmonger) and Elizabeth Fern. He was one of 11 children and the family lived in a small terraced house on Fenton Terrace, in the Stamp End area of Lincoln.

At 10am on Saturday, June 13th, 1868, Welcome (aged seven) asked his mother if he might be allowed to go out and play. Having been given permission, he called at the home of his eight-year-old friend Jim Scholefield, who lived nearby, and the two children embarked upon a crime spree. During the course of the morning, they stole a shilling, a chicken, some butter and other food items, from various unattended boats which were moored on the River Witham. As they walked along the bank towards the city centre they then came upon a barge owned by Thomas Simms. The two lads sneaked aboard and stole a pocket watch which had been left in plain sight.

The boys later approached a pork butcher on Silver Street and offered to sell him the watch for sixpence. Upon being questioned by the butcher, Welcome said that his mother had given him the watch. The butcher did not believe the story and sent for the police. Both boys confessed to their crimes and were charged with theft.

Welcome and Jim appeared before Magistrates at the City Police Court on Monday, June 15th, and pleaded Guilty. Mr R Hall JP, Chair of the bench, announced that the court were of the opinion that the best course of action would be to send the boys to the workhouse. When they heard this the mothers of both boys objected. After conferring, the Magistrates then announced that both boys would be kept in custody until 7pm that evening and that they would each receive a dozen strokes with a birch rod before being sent home.

What happened next?

On August 9th, 1877, Welcome (aged 15) entered an agreement to become a "bound apprentice" for a commercial fisherman, named Maddock, in Hull. Conditions were tough and he absconded just two months later. When caught, he was sentenced to 30 days imprisonment.

He subsequently returned to sea and the 1881 census shows he was the third hand on board The Diamond at Prince Albert Dock, in Hull. Sadly, on March 22nd, 1882, he was washed overboard and drowned. He was just 20 years old and his body was never found. Records relating to Jim Scholefield are inconclusive.

Primary source; Lincolnshire Chronicle, June 19th, 1868

Footnote:

Fishing remains one of the most dangerous jobs in the United Kingdom with 10 commercial fishermen having lost their lives in 2021. However, in Victorian times the job was even more perilous, especially for young deck hands. In the four-year period between 1878 and 1882, over 70 fisher-boys from the port of Hull alone, lost their lives to the sea.

13: George Seagrave

Lincoln - 1874: A Duel Between Schoolboys

George was born in 1861 to William (a farmer) and Charlotte Seagrave. The family were comparatively wealthy and lived at the Manor House in Lissington (near Wragby) along with several servants including a governess and a nurse. They also employed nine men and three boys to help farm their 342 acres of land.

By 1874 George had been enrolled at the Minster Yard Academy; a private boarding school in Lincoln, run by the Reverend Swift. The school was a very close knit community and most of the boys got along quite well, with one exception. Gerald Burn was the son of an architect in London and, for reasons unknown, he took an instant dislike to George.

On March 14th, 1874, Burn discovered that George had drawn a satirical cartoon which portrayed him in a negative light and, after a protracted quarrel, Burn challenged him to a duel. George accepted and they arranged to meet, along with their nominated seconds, in a meadow off Greetwell Road to settle the matter. At the appointed time, their seconds paced-out a distance of thirteen yards and hammered two stakes into the ground. The pistols were loaded with powder and a ball, and one was given to each boy. They then stood next to their respective stakes, took careful aim, and awaited the agreed signal.

A handkerchief was dropped, and the two boys discharged their weapons simultaneously. George's pistol made a muffled bang which resulted in the barrel bursting. Burn's pistol however, worked exactly as intended, and the projectile slammed into George's lower leg. He slumped to the ground clutching his bloody wound and screamed in pain. An improvised dressing was applied to the injury and he was carried back to school, where they sent for a doctor. The injury was not life-threatening but the bullet had smashed George's tibia and required complex surgery.

Maurice Burn was charged with "Shooting George Henry Seagrave with intent to cause grievous bodily harm" and appeared before Mr Baron Pollock, at the Lincoln Assizes, on March 17th, 1874. The court heard that the two pistols had been bought for sixpence each from Poppleton's Toy Shop in Lincoln. They were made from a metal similar to brass, with a primitive trigger, and originally had a cork with a string attached to it. The pistol was meant to be used with caps as a pop-gun, but Burn had made certain modifications which allowed them to be loaded with powder and ball projectiles. In his defence, Burn claimed that he never imagined the toy guns could cause such injury and he humbly apologised for what had happened.

The Jury returned a verdict of "Not Guilty," and the Judge issued him with a stern warning about his future conduct.

What happened next?

George made a full recovery and subsequently went to university to study medicine. He qualified as a doctor in 1887, and established a practice at Arnside, Westmoreland (now part of Cumbria). He married Mary Arnold in 1890, and the couple had two children. George died from natural causes at Thetford in 1908.

Gerald Burn settled in London where he married and had four children. He became a talented artist who specialised in painting large-scale nautical scenes. He exhibited at the Royal Academy and his work is displayed in several maritime museums across the country. He died in 1945, aged 86 years.

Primary source: Kentish Independent, March 21st, 1874

14: Rebecca Wheatley
Saxilby - 1877: Chained to a wall

Rebecca was born in Saxilby (6 miles west of Lincoln), and was baptised at St Botolph's Church in the village on August 28th, 1828. She was one of four children born to John (a farmer with 150 acres) and Sarah Wilkinson. She remained single until she was 30 years old, before marrying John Wheatley (a brewer) in May 1859. John's parents owned the Ship Inn at Saxilby and by 1871, John and Rebecca had taken over from his parents.

Rebecca had always enjoyed a drink but, by the autumn of 1877, she was drinking to excess on a daily basis, and had been brought before the Lindsey Magistrates, charged with drunkenness, on three separate occasions. By early November 1877, her craving for drink had developed to the point where she would snatch ale-glasses out of customers hands, and drink the contents in one go. John tried reasoning with her and she promised to curtail her drunkenness but, as soon as his back was turned, she would start drinking again. John decided to take decisive action, and he locked her in her bedroom with nothing but a glass of water for company. Rebecca went berserk; she smashed a chamber pot, threw a valuable lamp out of the window, and then smashed her way through the door to escape. In desperation, John sought advice from Doctor Rainbird who suggested that Rebecca should be "properly secured during these paroxysms."

By November 28th, 1877, Rebecca had been drinking almost continuously for eight or nine days and had become "bewildering". John sought the assistance of his brother, Thomas, to implement the doctor's advice. The two brothers overpowered Rebecca, dragged her upstairs, fastened a heavy chain around her body, and secured it to the wall with a padlock. Rebecca screamed and shouted all night, but was not released until 4pm the following afternoon, by which time she was in "a very indecent state."

Rebecca instructed a solicitor to summons John and Thomas for assaulting her, and they appeared before the Lindsey Magistrates on December 7th. Rebecca described her ordeal as "being kidnapped." She claimed that the chain was strong enough to hold an elephant and that she only had "A yard of liberty." John called two domestic servants and Doctor Rainbird in his defence, and they all testified to the effect that John had always been a good husband to Rebecca, and had never used any form of violence against her, despite extreme provocation on her part.

The court found there was no evidence against Thomas, but considered the case against John Wheatley to be proved. He was bound over, in his own recognisance, to keep the peace.

What happened next?

Between 1878 and 1883, there were at least three more convictions against Rebecca for being drunk in the street, or for being drunk on licensed premises. However, the couple remained together at the Ship Inn until John's death in 1901. Rebecca then spent the last years of her life living at Trinity House, on Bridge Street in Saxilby.

Rebecca, who never had any children, passed away in 1908 aged 79. She was buried in the graveyard of St Botolph's Church on February 10th, 1908. She chose not to be reunited with her husband in the afterlife, and was laid to rest in a separate grave.

Primary source: Stamford Mercury, December 14th, 1877

15: Henry Stebbings

Lincoln - 1879: An Epic Police Pursuit

Henry was born at Louth on June 2nd, 1852, to Edmund (a clog maker) and Sarah Ann Stebbings who lived on James Street in the town. The 1871 census shows that Henry was working as a clerk for a coal merchant in Louth, but by the time of his marriage to Rebekah Cole in 1876, he was a clerk for a firm of solicitors in Lincoln.

Henry was regarded as a highly-skilled administrator and his aptitude was rewarded in 1876 when he was appointed as Secretary for the Lincoln General Dispensary, where his responsibilities included paying invoices due and keeping accurate records. Rather foolishly, Henry started living beyond his means; the couple lived in a fine house (with servants) on Beaumont Fee, they wore expensive clothes and Henry indulged himself as a "bird and dog fancier".

By 1878, Henry was covering the shortfall in his income by "cooking the books" at work. He started small at first, but his method was always the same. He would wait until he received an invoice which needed paying, mark the invoice as "paid", make a corresponding entry in the cash book, and then pocket the money himself. Over successive months, the amount that he pilfered amounted to almost £600 (worth around £90,000 in today's money).

Following complaints from numerous suppliers demanding to know when they would actually receive their funds, the Chair of the committee called a meeting on October 30th, at which Henry was required to account for the discrepancies. Henry made some very convoluted excuses, but claimed he could account for every penny if the committee would allow him 24 hours to produce his books. The committee agreed.

Henry went straight home and confessed what he had been doing to Rebekah. He explained that he could not face the ignominy of being sent to prison. He told her that he was fleeing the country, and would send for her later. He packed his bags and caught an evening train to London. His movements over the following weeks are shrouded in mystery, but he subsequently booked a passage to New Zealand and boarded a sailing ship, named The Lorraine, at Gravesend, on November 21st, 1878.

Meanwhile, back in Lincoln, when Henry failed to appear at the re-convened meeting, the matter was reported to the city police. Detective Sergeant William Hockney was assigned to the case and circulated Henry's description, and photograph, to Police Forces across the country. On November 28th, Detective Sergeant Hockney received reliable information that Henry had boarded The Lorraine, and established that it was not scheduled to reach its destination until March 2nd, 1879. The officer then consulted shipping specialists and discovered that if he caught the steam ship, Somersetshire, from Gravesend on December 14th, then he would arrive in Wellington a few days before The Lorraine. Chief Constable Mansell made a short presentation to a hastily convened meeting of the General Dispensary Committee, who agreed to meet all reasonable costs for the officer to arrest Henry in New Zealand.

The Lorraine entered the port of Wellington on March 2nd, 1879. Then, as Henry Stebbings walked down the gangway, he was confronted by Detective Sergeant Hockney armed with a warrant for his arrest. Henry surrendered without a struggle. The pair left Wellington on March 20th on The Fernglen, and entered the Thames Estuary on July 2nd. After a police chase covering 30,000 miles, and lasting over 6 months, Henry was finally brought to justice when he appeared before Mr Justice Thesiger on July 19th, 1870, charged with forgery and fraud. He was found Guilty and sentenced to 5 years penal servitude.

What happened next?

The money pilfered by Henry Stebbings was never recovered and he was declared bankrupt in November 1878,

Henry served most of his sentence at HMP Chatham in Kent. Rebekah waited for him and the couple emigrated to South Africa shortly after his release in 1884. Rebecca sadly passed away at Uitenhage, in Eastern Cape province, in 1887 aged 35 years. It is not known what Henry did with his life over the next two decades, but records show that he died in Transvaal in November 1908.

Primary source: Lincolnshire Chronicle, December 20th, 1878

16: Dorothy Sparrow

Lincoln - 1881: Stabbed her Lover

Dorothy Matilda Sparrow was born in Branston in 1860. Her parents were Charles (a journeyman blacksmith) and Mary. The family lived at 2, Back Lane, in the village, and Dorothy was the eldest of seven children. Very little is known about her childhood except that she left Branston as a teenager and moved to Lincoln. She fell upon hard times and her life descended into one of bawdy drunkenness. Local newspapers provided some clues about the lifestyle she was leading. On November 21st, 1879, she appeared before the Magistrates charged with being a "common prostitute". She was imprisoned for seven days. Then, on February 27th, 1880, she was fined 10 Shillings for disorderly conduct on Waterside North.

At 9:30pm on Monday, May 2nd, 1881, Constable Lacey was on patrol on Lincoln High Street when he heard a commotion coming from the direction of the Ship Inn on Waterside North. When he arrived, he saw Dorothy leaning against the railings. She complained of having been assaulted by a man named Jonathan Arnold, who had kicked her about her legs and body, and she wanted him locked up. The officer entered the premises and saw Arnold, slumped in a chair, bleeding profusely from a wound near his left ear. Arnold claimed he did not know what had happened but another customer told the officer that he had seen Dorothy stab Arnold with a long-pointed knife. The officer sent for Doctor Harrison to attend to Arnold before arresting Dorothy. She was placed in a cell overnight.

Dorothy appeared at the Sessions House the following morning where the Magistrates heard evidence from various witnesses. Arnold seemed reluctant to testify but said that he had met Dorothy some five weeks previously and they had been living together at 34, Park Street. He went on to say that after having a trivial argument with Dorothy at the inn, he suddenly found he was bleeding heavily from his head, but he did not know what had caused it.

The Magistrates then heard from John Wheatcroft, a labourer living at 20, Spital Street, who said he was drinking with Arnold in the Ship Inn when Dorothy came in. She accused Arnold of cavorting with another woman, and said that she would sort him out before the night was out. A boatman, named Samuel Humphrey, then testified that he saw the pair come out of the Ship Inn together when Dorothy suddenly reached under her shawl and produced a knife. Then without saying another word, she quickly stabbed Arnold two or three times below his left ear. Doctor Harrison then testified that the wounds were very deep and one of them was perilously close to a major artery. The Magistrates indicted Dorothy and released her on bail to appear at the next Quarter Sessions. Over the next few weeks Dorothy engineered a reconciliation with Arnold and the pair married at Lincoln Registry Office in June, 1881.

When Dorothy appeared at the Quarter Sessions on July 2nd, 1881, she pleaded Not Guilty to the charge of wounding. She put forward a defence that they had both been drinking and that Arnold had attacked her first. Arnold then took advantage of a law (which prevailed at the time) under which a married person could not be compelled to give evidence against their spouse. However, after hearing from the other witnesses the Jury returned a verdict of, "Guilty." In passing sentence, the Judge remarked that he was inclined to be lenient and imprisoned Dorothy for one month with hard labour.

What happened next?

After her release Dorothy found that Arnold had left the city without leaving word of his intentions, so she joined other women at a brothel in "The Drapery" (a slum area between Michaelgate and Steep Hill). On Friday, November 18th, 1881, Dorothy was found Guilty of stealing 4 Shillings from William Fletcher, a farmer from Norton Disney. It seems that Fletcher fell asleep whilst being "entertained" so Dorothy helped herself to the contents of his purse. She was imprisoned for seven days with hard labour.

By the beginning of 1882, Dorothy had moved to Boston where she tried to start a new life. She was mentioned in the Boston Guardian in March 1885, when she was fined a shilling for being drunk outside the Nags Head Inn. It was reported that she lived at 26, Pinfold Lane, and took in other people's washing to make ends meet.

Dorothy died in Boston, from natural causes, in 1899 aged 38 years.

Primary source: Lincolnshire Chronicle 8th July 1881

17: Lewis Kirby

1884 - Branston: A Perverted Curate

Lewis was baptised in Kent in 1858 and was one of six children born to William (a vicar) and Mary Kirby. The family moved to Bloomsbury (North London) in 1862, and then to Cheshunt, Hertfordshire, in 1871. After leaving school, Lewis studied theology at university, and took Holy Orders in 1880. His first substantive appointment was at St Andrew's College, Bloemfontein, South Africa, where he met Beatrice White (who was originally from Grantham). They married at Bloemfontein Cathedral on August 27th, 1882. For reasons which have not been documented, the couple returned to England, and on March 1st, 1884, Lewis was appointed as a licensed curate in the parish of Branston, near Lincoln.

During the evening of Friday, December 5th, 1884, the Reverend Kirby drove his pony and trap to the schoolroom at Branston Fen, where he was scheduled to give some form of theatrical entertainment to the local children. Shortly after his arrival, he sat down upon a bench and put his arms around the waist of two young girls. He then took the hand of 11-year-old Rebecca King, and asked her if she would like to see his pony. After encouraging her to stroke the animal, he ushered her into a nearby coach-house, where he placed her on his knee. He then started kissing Rebecca and proceeded to "put filthy questions to her, and committed acts of a most disgusting kind." He gave Rebecca two pennies, and told her to say nothing about what had happened.

Rebecca held her silence until the following Wednesday when she confided her secret to two other girls in her class. Later that day one of the girls informed their teacher, who in turn informed the Rural Dean, Canon Perry. The following day, Lewis Kirby went to the house at Fen Head where Rebecca lived with her Aunt

Phoebe. Lewis apologised to Phoebe for what he had done to Rebecca, and begged forgiveness.

Forgiveness was not forthcoming however, and the Reverend Kirby was summonsed to appear before the Kesteven Magistrates on Friday, January 9th, 1885, charged with having, "Indecently assaulted, and ill-treated Rebecca King, eleven years of age." Kirby entered a plea of Not Guilty. The case for the prosecution was outlined by Mr Tweed, who said he would call witnesses who could testify about the way in which Kirby had put his arms around two girls before taking Rebecca into the coach house, and he would also call Phoebe Speed, who could say that Kirby admitted to having committed the act.

Mr Williams, who was representing Kirby, pointed out that the Magistrates would be unable to deal with the serious matter before them and it would have to be referred to the Assizes. He then went on to suggest that, if the charge was reduced to one of having "Unlawfully committed an aggravated assault upon Rebecca King," then his client would plead Guilty. After conferring, the Magistrates agreed to this course of action. Canon Perry gave a character reference saying that Kirby had "Worked hard and zealously in the parish." In passing sentence, the Chair of the Bench informed Kirby that he had narrowly avoided being sent to prison, and fined him £20.

What happened next?

The 1891 census shows that Rebecca King was working as a domestic servant for the Watson family on Monks Road, Lincoln. She married a man named George Miller at Gainsborough in 1893, but she died from natural causes in March 1897, aged 23. She was laid to rest in Canwick Road Cemetery, Lincoln.

Lewis Kirby resigned his position as curate and pursued a new career as an actor with Mr Charles Dornton's Theatrical Company. He adopted the stage name of Lewis Coghlan and, by 1888, he was touring the country playing a character called Elijah Coomb in a production called "The Silver King". In October

1888 he contracted pneumonia whilst performing at Berwick upon Tweed. He did not respond to treatment and passed away on October 30th, 1888, aged 30.

Newly widowed Beatrice Kirby was soon to suffer another tragedy. In January 1890, their only child, Gladys Isabel Mary Kirby (aged two), passed away at Brighton. However, Beatrice subsequently found happiness with a man named Johnson Oates. The couple married in London in 1891, and they went on to have a child of their own. Beatrice passed away in Shoreditch in 1939, aged 69.

Primary source: Spalding Guardian, January 10th, 1885

18: Richard Atkinson

Heighington - 1887: Reckless Curiosity

Most official records agree that Richard was born in 1847. Some show that he was born in Washingborough (e.g., 1901 Census) but the 1911 Census indicates he was born at Eaton, Leicestershire. Consequently, the first three decades of his life are difficult to unravel.

However, by 1881, he was working as an agricultural labourer in Heighington, near Lincoln, when he was pelted with stones by a 12-year-old youth called Frederick Turnhill. One of the stones caused a nasty head injury and the matter was reported to the police. Frederick appeared at the Kesteven Petty Sessions on December 2nd charged with assault. During the proceedings the court heard that Richard Atkinson was, "A half-witted young fellow, and the lads of the village were constantly bullying him." Frederick was fined 5 shillings.

At 2:27pm, on Wednesday, September 28th, 1887, an express train was travelling through Heighington at a speed of 60mph. As it passed under a bridge, the driver heard a loud bang when the engine hit a large stone which had been placed on the line. As luck would have it, the stone was deflected by the protective guard-iron at the front of the engine, and the train was able to continue its journey to Doncaster.

At 4:15pm the same day, a platelayer called John Banyard was walking along the track and, as he passed under the bridge, he saw a large stone lying between the rails, and moved it to a gully at the side of the track. Mr Banyard then noticed that his actions were being observed by Richard Atkinson who was working in an adjacent field, and they had a short conversation about when the next train was due to pass. Mr Banyard reported the incident when he returned to Branston station, and mentioned that he had seen Richard in the immediate vicinity.

The following day, William Linton (Station Master at Branston) and Constable Brackenbury visited the scene. They examined the large stone and saw that it was partially covered in moss, and that it was deeply scored where it had been struck by the engine. PC Brackenbury noticed that Richard was working nearby and asked him, "Dick, have you put a stone on the railway?" Richard replied, "I did not do it on purpose. I kicked it with my foot, and it rolled down accidentally". The officer then asked Richard to show him where the stone was before it was dislodged. Richard took the officer to a spot high on an embankment some 25 yards away, and pointed to a depression in the earth which corresponded in shape and size with the large stone. The large stone was subsequently recovered and found to weigh 60 pounds (27 kg).

Over the next few days, police officers and railway officials conducted experiments at the scene in an attempt to establish whether Richard's explanation was plausible. Several large stones were rolled down the embankment from the spot indicated by Richard but, on each occasion, the stones came to rest on a level terrace half way down the slope.

Richard Atkinson was arrested on October 5th, 1887, and taken to the county police station in Lincoln where he was cautioned and charged with "Feloniously and maliciously placing a stone upon the line with intent to upset and overthrow a certain engine, tender and carriages, used on that railway." In reply to the charge Richard said, "I will tell the truth. I pulled it up with my hands, and rolled it down the bank. I then went down and put it against the metals [rails], but I never meant a bit of harm. I just wanted to see what it would do. I did it when I went back to dinner, and this is the first time I have done such a thing."

Richard Atkinson appeared before Mr Justice Hudlestone at the Nottingham Winter Assizes on November 10th, 1887, and pleaded Guilty. Before sentence was passed, the court heard from Dr G Mitchinson who testified that, in his opinion, Richard Atkinson was "Of unsound mind, and not capable of understanding the proceedings at court, and incapable of defending himself." His Lordship ordered that Richard Atkinson should be "Confined during her Majesty's pleasure"

What happened next?

A Criminal Lunacy Warrant was issued by the court authorising Richard's removal to the County Lunatic Asylum at Nottingham. On February 6th, 1897, he was transferred to the Kesteven Lunatic Asylum (later known as Rauceby Hospital) where he remained for the rest of his life.

He passed away on February 22nd, 1924 aged 76 years.

Primary sources:
Lincolnshire Chronicle: October 14th, 1887
Lincolnshire Chronicle: December 9th, 1881
UK Lunacy Patients Admission Registers, 1846-1921

19: John Hickey

Lincoln - 1888: A Fight for a Woman

John was born in Boston, in 1862, to Patrick (a traveling draper) and Ann Hickey. By 1871 the family had moved to 18, Bethel Place (off St Mary Street), Lincoln.

John started getting into trouble with the police as a teenager and had his first taste of prison in 1881, when he was sentenced to 21 days with hard labour for stealing sixpence. Over the next six years he made numerous appearances at court; he was fined for brawling in the street on eight occasions, and sent to prison four times for theft, disorderly conduct and using obscene language.

By 1888 John had developed feelings for a woman named Elizabeth Baldwin from Coultham Street. Elizabeth was married, but lived apart from her husband (a musician named William Baldwin), and earned her living as a prostitute.

Around midnight on Saturday, June 23rd, 1888, John found Elizabeth at a public house in the company of man named Thomas Hanold from Hungate Court. John became agitated and demanded that Elizabeth should come away with him. Heated words and threats of violence were exchanged between the two men, who both made declarations of undying love for the woman.

Elizabeth was both flattered and amused by this contest for her affection, but was unable to choose between her two suitors. It then occurred to Elizabeth that there was only one way to settle the argument; she announced that the two men should fight it out, and the better man could have her. It was then mutually agreed that the "prize fight" would take place at Holmes Common at 1am.

The two men met as arranged, but rumours of the event had spread throughout the city and a crowd of around one hundred people gathered to witness the spectacle. The two men stripped to the waist and started exchanging punishing blows over several rounds. John was clearly winning the fight when it was suddenly interrupted by local police officers. The two men fled the scene, leaving their clothes behind. John however, was recognised by the officers and was later summonsed to appear at court. When he appeared before the Magistrates, John promised not to repeat the offence and was bound-over to keep the peace for 3 months.

What happened next?

Elizabeth claimed her "prize" and took John as her lover. They funded their lifestyle by committing petty crime. On the 9th of October 1889, they both appeared at the Lincoln Quarter Sessions charged with stealing a pocket watch from an elderly gentleman that they had befriended in a city centre pub. Elizabeth was sentenced to 12 months imprisonment with hard labour. John was sentenced to five years penal servitude.

By 1891, Elizabeth Baldwin was living in Gainsborough where she formed a relationship with a labourer named Thomas Lawrence. The relationship ended violently in March 1901, when Lawrence tried to cut her throat with a pocket knife before bashing her about her head and knocking out one of her teeth. She made a full recovery but passed away in Gainsborough in 1909, aged 50.

The 1891 census shows that John Hickey was incarcerated at Portland Prison in Dorset. It would appear that he emigrated to the United States shortly after his release but records of his life beyond this point are inconclusive.

Primary source; Stamford Mercury, 29th June, 1888

20: Percy Blow

Lincoln -1889: Heroic City Footballer

Edward Percy Blow (always known as Percy, or Corkie) made over 162 appearances for Lincoln City Football Club between 1901 and 1906. However, it was his exploits off the pitch which earned him an award for bravery.

Percy was born in Lincoln on November 16th, 1877, to Thomas (a wheelwright) and Annie Blow. He was the second eldest of nine children who lived in a terraced house at 7, Sidney Street (off Bargate), Lincoln.

During the afternoon of Tuesday, January 8th, 1889, hundreds of people made their way to Mr Shepherd's field at Bracebridge. The Witham had spilled its banks a few days earlier covering the field with a couple of inches of water. Extreme cold weather then froze the water and offered the opportunity of ice skating in complete safety. Amongst the skaters were two brothers named Willie and John Bray from Russell Street. They spent a few hours sliding on the ice before deciding to return home. However, instead of making their way to the nearest bridge, they decided they would take a shorter route directly across the frozen river. The two brothers, along with another lad named Taylor, proceeded very cautiously and joined hands as they edged across. Taylor crossed the river safely, but the ice suddenly gave way pitching the two brothers into deep water. Taylor shouted for help.

Percy Blow (then aged 11) was nearby, together with a lad named Barton. When they heard the shout they made their way to the water's edge. Realising the danger, Percy gingerly made his way onto the ice, and adopted a spread-eagled posture to spread his weight. Barton took hold of Percy's ankle in case the ice broke. Percy managed to grab John Bray's hand and successfully rescued him from the icy water. Sadly, young Willie had disappeared from view before Percy arrived.

Someone ran to the police station at South Park and PC Kempshall rushed to the scene with a drag line. He commandeered a boat and started smashing the ice in an attempt to find the boy. The search continued until nightfall, but Willie could not be found. Over the next two weeks the ice melted and water levels dropped. Willie's body was eventually recovered on January 21st, some 400 yards from the spot where he entered the water. A Coroner's Inquest returned a verdict of "Accidental death."

In March, 1889, Percy Blow was presented with a bronze medal by the Royal Humane Society for his brave action in rescuing John Bray.

What happened next?

Willie was the 9-year-old son of Elijah (a foundry labourer) and Maria Bray who lived on nearby Russell Street. Details of where he was buried have not been established.

John Bray, who was rescued by Percy, became a blacksmith and married Rose Johnson in 1910. They lived at 17, Frances Street, Bracebridge, from 1911 until the day John died in 1949 aged 68.

After leaving school, Percy Blow worked as a joiner until he signed as a professional footballer for Lincoln City FC. He made his debut during the last match of the 1900-01 season and became a regular member of the first team for the next five years, playing at left-half. He married Mildred Turner in 1915 and they would eventually have eight children. He joined the Royal Engineers in April 1915 and served through The Great War in France. Luckily, he was unscathed during the conflict and he was discharged from the service in 1918.

He died in London in 1938 aged 60, and was laid to rest in Hendon Cemetery.

Primary Source; Stamford Mercury, January 25th, 1889.

21: Anna Bell

Lincoln - 1891: Poisonous Medication

Anna was born in Lincoln in 1858 to Charles (a stonemason) and Eliza Downs. She was the youngest of four children and the family lived at 6, St Benedict's Square, Lincoln. Tragically, Anna's father passed away shortly before she was born, and Eliza raised the children single-handedly. Anna went into service as a teenager, and the 1881 census shows she was a housekeeper to the Newbold family who lived at 14, St Benedict's Square.

During the autumn of 1881, Anna married Douglas Malcolm Bell (an auctioneer's clerk), and children soon followed. Between 1882 and 1888 she gave birth to four children, and her fifth child, Jessie, was born in February, 1892.

By January 1893, the family were living at 8, St Benedict's Square, and the children contracted measles. The older children had a mild form of the illness but baby Jessie was quite poorly and Anna took her to see Doctor Pedroza at the Monks Road Friendly Society Dispensary, on Monday, January 9th. The doctor prescribed some medicine to be taken orally, and some liniment to soothe the rash.

Jessie had a very troubled night, and woke up crying several times. Shortly after midnight Anna got out of bed to tend to her, and rubbed some of the liniment on her rash. Jessie woke again at 3:30am in a very irritable state, and Anna decided to give her half a teaspoonful of the oral medicine. She reached for the bottle from the mantlepiece and administered it to the child. Then, as she replaced the bottle, she suddenly realised that she had mistakenly given Jessie some of the liniment. She awoke Douglas to inform him what had happened.

The couple decided that, despite it being very early in the morning, that they would fetch a doctor immediately. Douglas initially went to Doctor Lambert's premises on Cornhill, but could not raise anyone. He then went to Doctor Pedroza's residence, arriving shortly after 4am. The doctor told Douglas that he should return home straight away and try to get the child to vomit, keep her awake, and keep her feet warm. The doctor added that he would call first thing in the morning to check on Jessie.

Douglas and Anna managed to make Jessie vomit, and followed the doctor's other instructions to the letter, but Jessie's breathing became very laboured and she fell asleep for the last time shortly before Doctor Pedroza attended the house at 9:30am.

A Coroner's Inquest was held on Wednesday, January 11th, where Douglas and Anna related the events leading up to Jessie's death. The Jury then heard from Doctor Pedroza who said he had been with another patient, on Thomas Street, until the early hours of the morning and had only just got to bed when Mr Bell called at his house. He went on to say that the advice he gave to Mr Bell was medically sound, and even if he had attended to Jessie himself he could not have done anything different for the child. He also testified that the liniment which Jessie had been given contained a highly toxic blend of opium, belladonna (deadly nightshade), aconite and chloroform. It was, undoubtedly, what caused the child's death. In addressing the Jury the Coroner said he thought "The mother was a witness of truth, who had sadly made a simple mistake." The Jury returned a verdict of "Death from misadventure".

What happened next?

Jessie was laid to rest in plot C793, at Canwick Road Old Cemetery, on January 13th, 1893. She was just 11 months old.

Anna became pregnant with her 6th child during the summer of 1896, and she went into labour on March 26th, 1897. The delivery was difficult, and Anna sadly died from complications the following day. Her baby, named Malcolm after his father, sadly passed away a few days later. Anna, aged 38 years, and baby Malcolm, both share their grave with Jessie.

Douglas engaged the services of various housekeepers to help him raise the other children. In later life, he bought a house on Newark Road, North Hykeham. Douglas went on to have a long life, and passed away in October, 1933 aged 81.

Primary source; Lincolnshire Chronicle, January 13th, 1893.

22: Maud Hunt

Lincoln - 1891: Burglar with a Bayonet

Maud Marion Hunt was born at Trimulgherry, India, on September 18th, 1870, to Henry (an officer in the British Army) and Hannah Hunt. She had five siblings who were born between 1866 and 1875 at various locations across the British Empire. By 1890 her father had been promoted to Captain Quartermaster in the 3rd Battalion of the Lincolnshire Regiment, and the family lived in quarters at Sobraon Barracks on Burton Road, Lincoln. Maud shared a bedroom with her two sisters.

John Burns, aged 21, was a powerfully built man who was originally from 12, Mill Street, Hull. He was recruited into the 3rd Battalion of the Lincolnshire Regiment at the beginning of 1891, and was posted to Sobraon Barracks. During the early hours of Friday, April 2nd, 1891, Burns sneaked out of his quarters and made his way to the staff-paymaster's office. He then used his bayonet in an attempt to force entry, but the sturdy door resisted his efforts, so he looked for an easier target.

At 2am, Maud was awoken from her sleep by the sound of faint rustling from within the bedroom. She whispered to her older sister, "There's someone in the room," and the rustling stopped. Maud then raised her voice and said, "If you don't identify yourself I will ring the electric bell." All three sisters then started screaming loudly and the intruder left hurriedly. Henry Hunt was awakened by the sound of his daughters' screams and rushed to their room. Maud told her father what had happened and he then left to search for the culprit.

Moments later, Maud heard her father shout, "I've got him; bring a light." Maud rushed out of the room with a lamp and found her father grappling with Burns. The two men rolled down the stairway and ended up in a half-kneeling position facing each other in the hallway. Burns shouted, "I'll do for you." At that point Maude saw that Burns had a bayonet in his hand and immediately realised that her father was in mortal danger. Maude rushed down the last few steps and unsuccessfully tried to wrench the bayonet out of Burns' hand. Maude then picked up a heavy set of coal tongs and administered several hard blows to Burns' head. Burns groaned and slumped to the floor. He still had hold of the bayonet and, when he then tried to sit up, Maud gave him two more blows which rendered him senseless.

Soldiers on guard nearby had heard the commotion and took Burns into custody. Maud saw that her father was bleeding from several wounds and rendered first aid until medical assistance arrived. Burns was brought before magistrates the following morning and remanded in custody. He was subsequently sentenced to five years penal servitude.

What happened next?

Henry Hunt made a full recovery from his injuries and Maud's bravery was acclaimed in newspapers across the country. She was presented with a commemorative photograph album by the Mayor of Lincoln, and with a gold brooch, known as the Victoria Wreath, by the proprietors of the Gentlewoman Magazine.

Maud married a wealthy solicitor called Walter Standring in 1896 and the couple had two children. She went on to have a long life before passing away in Warwick in 1958 aged 87.

Records relating to John Burns are inconclusive.

Primary source; Stamford Mercury, April 10th, 1891

23: Eliza Ann Luff

Lincoln 1893: A Dying Declaration?

Eliza was born at Sheffield in 1867 and was the eldest of eight children whose parents were Samuel (a foundry worker) and Sarah Grocutt. The 1881 census shows that by the time Eliza was 14, the family had moved to 23, Anchor Street, Lincoln. In March 1884, she married a foundry worker named Harry Luff (sometimes given as Laff). The couple made their home on Clarkson's Row (off High Street, near the Shakespeare Inn), and their first child was born six months later.

By the end of December 1892, the couple were living at 39, Mill Lane, Lincoln, and they had four young children. Christmas was a happy affair, but by the beginning of January 1893 Eliza realised that she was in the early stages of another pregnancy.

On Monday, January 9th, 1893, Eliza told Harry that she was going to the local shop to buy some groceries. She was away from the house for less than an hour, but when she returned she looked very ill. She told Harry that she felt a bit queasy and complained of pain in the lower part of her body. By the following Monday, Eliza's condition had deteriorated to the point that she was unable to get out of bed without assistance, and Harry sent for Doctor Wigham. The doctor suspected that Eliza had peritonitis (see footnote) and prescribed some medicine. However, when the doctor returned on Thursday, January 19th, he discovered that Eliza had not taken any of the medication and he told Harry that he would not come to the house again. Later the same morning, Eliza started bleeding heavily between her legs so Harry sent for Doctor Howse. After a brief examination, he realised that Eliza had had a miscarriage. He treated her accordingly and suggested that someone should sit with her day and night.

At 5:15pm on Saturday afternoon, Eliza spoke to her husband and said, "Harry, fetch Doctor Howse. Go now, or I shall be dead before you get back." A neighbour, called Emily Blow, kept Eliza company until the doctor arrived at 9pm. By this time Eliza was gravely ill and, despite the doctor's best efforts, Eliza passed away shortly after midnight.

A Coroner's Inquest was held at the Blue Anchor Hotel the following Monday and the Jury heard evidence from three doctors who had performed a post mortem examination. They all agreed that Eliza had passed away as a result of internal injuries caused by an instrument that had been inserted by an unskilled person. They went onto say that some considerable force had been used and that the injuries could not have been self-inflicted.

The Jury then heard from Emily Blow, who had sat with Eliza whilst Harry went to fetch the doctor. Emily told the Coroner's Jury that Eliza had confided that she had visited a woman named Caroline Sharpe, to try to get rid of the baby. On the first visit she was given some pills to take but, when they failed to produce the desired effect, she returned to the house on Monday, January 9th. On the second visit Mrs Sharpe "Went to a set of drawers and removed something which was wrapped in a handkerchief." Eliza went on to describe how much it hurt when the instrument was placed inside her and said, "Oh, Emm, Emm, I shall die. Mrs Sharpe has killed me." After due consideration, the Coroner's Jury returned a verdict of "Wilful Murder," by Caroline Sharpe.

Police Sergeant Wells went to Caroline Sharpe's home at 401, High Street, Lincoln, the following day and said, "Mrs Sharpe, I am going to apprehend you on a charge of feloniously causing the death of Eliza Ann Luff by performing an illegal operation with intent to procure an abortion on the 9th of the present month." Mrs Sharpe replied, "Very well; it's very hard for a woman bringing up children without a friend in the world." She was brought before the Magistrates the following day and remanded in custody.

Caroline Sharpe (a dressmaker) appeared before Mr Justice Day at the Lincoln Assizes on February 25th, 1893. In opening the case for the prosecution, Mr Harris QC summarised the evidence against the defendant, during which he conceded that the conversation which Eliza had with Emma Blow was "hearsay", because it was not made in the presence of the accused person. However, he then went on to argue that, as Eliza had expressed her fear that she was about to die, then the evidence should be admitted as a dying declaration (see footnote).

Caroline Sharpe was represented by Mr Fox QC who pointed out that, apart from the statement which Eliza allegedly made to Emma Blow, there was not a shred of evidence to link his client with Eliza Luff's death. He then argued that, for hearsay evidence to be admissible as a dying declaration, there must be, "A settled and hopeless expectation of impending death." He submitted that, as Eliza had sent for a doctor, she must have had some hope of recovery, and the hearsay evidence should therefore be inadmissible. The Judge agreed with Mr Fox's submission. The case collapsed, and Caroline Sharpe walked away as a free woman.

What happened next?

Eliza Luff was laid to rest in plot B3248, at Canwick Road Old Cemetery. She was 26 years old.

On May 24th, 1893, Harry Luff boarded the Lord Clive with his eldest 2 children and sailed for America. Immigration records in the USA show that he had £6 in his pocket when he arrived, and that he planned to stay with his aunt, Mrs Plant, who lived on Kirkwood Street, Pittsburgh. It is probable that his youngest two children were being looked after by a relative in England but, in any event, Harry came back for them in August, 1895, and took them to America. Details of the family's life beyond this point are inconclusive.

The 1911 census shows that Caroline Sharpe was living at 67, Princess Street, Lincoln. She died in 1916, aged 62, and was buried in plot B1322 at Canwick Road Old Cemetery,

Primary Source: Nottinghamshire Guardian, January 28th, 1893

Footnotes:

Peritonitis is an inflammation of the tissue which forms the inner wall of the abdomen.

A dying declaration is testimony which would normally be excluded on the grounds that it was hearsay. However, it may be admitted as evidence in criminal law trials if they were the words of a dying person. The rationale being that, if a person believes that death is imminent, they would have less incentive to fabricate their testimony, and as such, the hearsay testimony is more likely to be reliable.

24: Walter Green

Lincoln - 1894: Rescued, but...

Walter was born in Lincoln in 1883. He was the eldest of three children born to John (a groom) and Rosa Green who lived at 3, Hall's Yard, Lincoln. Access to the yard was by way of a narrow passage on Waterside South, directly opposite the Green Dragon.

Sunday, December 2nd, 1894 was a cold winter's day, but Walter was determined to make the best of a day off school, and spent the morning playing in the nearby streets with his friends. He went out again after lunch and met up with his friend, James Cunnington, who lived at 1, Hall's Yard. The two lads made their way along the banks of the Witham, towards Stamp End.

By 5pm, it was almost completely dark. Police Sergeant Dawson and Constable Milner were both standing on the bridge near the Green Dragon, when they heard a voice shout, "There's someone in the river!" The officers ran towards Doughty's Mill and came upon a man named Charles Crane, of Bagholme Road. Mr Crane was pointing excitedly towards a boy who was splashing about in the water a few yards from the bank. PC Milner and Mr Crane commandeered a small boat, which was tied up alongside a barge, and swiftly rescued Walter from the water. Upon reaching the bank, Sergeant Dawson asked, "What happened?" Walter replied, "I was leaning over the railings and I fell in." When the officer then asked if anyone else was in the water, Walter said, "No." The boy was clearly very cold as a result of his immersion, but otherwise seemed to be unharmed. The officers took Walter home and he was promptly put to bed.

It was not unusual for James Cunnington to stay out late and his father, William, was not unduly concerned until he heard about Walter's rescue from the water. Mr Cunnington then made his way to the police station at 7pm, and reported his concerns that James might also be in the river.

Sergeant Dawson and PC Milner made their way back to the river, but could see nothing untoward from either bank. They then made a search of the barge itself and found 2 boy's caps at the front end of the vessel. They then used a drag line and sadly recovered James' body from the deep water at the side of the barge shortly after 9pm. Doctor Harrison pronounced that life had been extinct for some time.

A Coroner's Inquest was held at the Sessions House the following afternoon. Evidence of identification was given by Mr Cunnington, and the two police officers described their own involvement in the incident. Walter Green then testified that he had gone onto the barge with James, and had fallen into the river whilst leaning over the railings. James then tried to rescue Walter, but fell into the river himself, and sank beneath the surface before the two police officers arrived. The Coroner then asked Walter why he did not tell the truth to the police at the time. Walter replied, "I was so frightened that I forgot to mention it." After due consideration, the Coroner's Jury returned a verdict of "Accidental death."

What happened next?

James Cunnington was laid to rest in plot 0470, at St Swithin's Cemetery, on December 5th, 1894. He was just 8 years old.

The 1901 census shows that Walter Green was still living at 3, Hall's Yard, and that he was working as a carter for a corn merchant. Details of his life beyond this point are inconclusive.

Primary source; Lincolnshire Chronicle, December 4th, 1894

25: Dick Elderkin

Lincoln - 1895: Mauled by a Mad Dog

Dick was born on August 8th, 1889, to William (a baker) and Emily Elderkin. He was one of five children and the family lived above their bakery at the junction of Bailgate and Gordon Road in Lincoln.

During the afternoon of June 21st, 1895, six-year-old Dick was playing in the street on St Paul's Lane, when he was suddenly confronted by a snarling dog. He backed away slowly but the dog leapt up at him and attacked his head "in a most frightful manner, with his scalp being literally torn off." Dick ran home crying, with his scalp hanging on by a small flap of skin. His mother sent for Doctor Sympson who anaesthetised Dick with chloroform and skilfully stitched it back in place.

Earlier that day, at 10am in the morning, a farmer named William Carter had been out shepherding with his dog at Bucknall, when it began acting very strangely and ran off towards Bardney. Over the course of the next few hours, it attacked a 16-year-old lad at Tupholme, and four children in Bardney. It then made its way across the fields to Short Ferry where it bit a 5-year-old boy. About an hour later it attacked an 8-year-old girl in Nettleham, before heading towards Lincoln. The dog attacked four other dogs in the vicinity of Greetwell Road, and then made its way towards Bailgate.

After attacking Dick Elderkin, the dog bolted into a narrow passageway leading to the Castle Mount, and was shot dead by a man named Frank Seely. The dog's body was examined by a veterinary surgeon who suspected it had rabies. He sent its head to a laboratory in London and received a report by telegram the following day confirming his suspicions.

With eight injured children at risk of contracting rabies themselves, a public subscription was organised by Mr Burnett of Bailgate, and Mr Sharpe from Bardney, to raise enough money to send the children to the Pasteur Institute in Paris which was, at that time, the world's leading authority on vaccination and inoculation.

Their financial target was reached quickly, and on Tuesday, June 25th, a special train arrived at the Great Northern Station in Lincoln. One of the carriages was equipped with beds and medical equipment which might be required for the journey. All eight injured children were brought aboard, together with Doctor Sympson, a nurse, and Mr Sharpe. Dick's mother, Emily, was allowed to accompany him throughout the journey. The train arrived at Dover at 8:15pm that evening and reached Paris at 5:40am the following morning, where the children were then transferred to the institute for treatment.

What happened next?

The treatment was successful. The children returned to their homes two weeks later, and none of them developed rabies.

After leaving school, Dick Elderkin worked for his father as a carter. He developed a passion for horses and, in his early twenties, he was employed at Lord Yarborough's Racing Stables. In his spare time he enjoyed playing cricket at the Lindum Cricket Club. However, when war was declared against Germany in 1914, he was amongst the first to volunteer. He was assigned to the 16th (The Queen's) Lancers Regiment and was sent to France in February 1915. He had a narrow escape shortly after his arrival, when three German mines exploded beneath the trenches being held by his regiment. On that day, 56 of his colleagues were killed, wounded or reported missing, but Dick was unscathed.

On April 7th, 1917, Dick's parents received a postcard from their son saying that he was alive and well. Sadly, just seven days later, they received a telegram from the Regimental Chaplain saying that he had been injured in combat and had died from his wounds.

Dick was 27 years old and had never married. He was buried alongside his fallen comrades at the Duisans British Cemetery in Northern France. Dick is commemorated on the large memorial in Lincoln City Centre, and on a white marble plaque in St Mary Magdalene's Church on Bailgate.

Primary source; Boston Guardian, June 29th, 1895

26: Nathan Bagley

Lincoln - 1902: Died for Love

Nathan was born in Lincoln in August 25th, 1881, and was one of 5 sons born to Joseph (a stonemason) and Hannah Bagley. His baptism records show that his given names were James Nathaniel Bagley, but he was always known as Nathan. The family lived at 40, Hungate, Lincoln, during Nathan's early childhood, but moved to 2, Eden Place (off Melville Street), when he was in his early teens. After leaving school, he gained employment as a foundry labourer and took lodgings with the Hodson family at 61, Ripon Street, Lincoln.

Hannah Ellison Denton, who preferred to be known as Ella, was the 23-year-old daughter of Arthur (a carpenter) and Fanny Denton of 64, King Street, Lincoln. It is thought that she met Nathan during the Christmas celebrations of 1900, and by January 1901, they had started walking out together. Over the course of the following months Nathan was invited for tea at the Denton's home most weekends, and by January 1902, the couple considered themselves to be informally engaged.

Nathan eventually plucked up the courage to ask Arthur Denton for his daughter's hand in marriage when he went for tea on Saturday, April 19th, 1902. The discussion did not go well. Whilst Arthur did not specifically say, "No," he made it quite clear that he would prefer his daughter to marry a man who had a proper trade. Nathan was heartbroken and stormed out of the house in a bad mood.

Nathan arranged to see Ella again on Wednesday, April 23rd. He thought it best not to call at the house, so they met at the end of a nearby passage at 6:30pm. The couple walked to South Common and spent much of the evening in silence. As the time approached for the couple to part, Ella said, "My father was never in favour of you, but I don't need his permission to marry you; I am old enough to decide for myself." Nathan then flourished two bullets from his pocket and said, "This will finish it all. Goodnight." Then, without uttering another word, he turned and walked away into the darkness.

Shortly after 10pm, a man named William Wilkinson was walking near St Andrew's Cricket Ground, when he heard the sound of a gunshot nearby. He went to investigate and found the body of a young man, lying motionless, near the railway bridge at the end of Sewell's Walk. As he got closer, he saw a small pool of blood near the man's head, and found a revolver on the ground next to him. Mr Wilkinson picked up the gun and went to find a policeman.

At 10:15pm, Constable Calvert was patrolling his beat on High Street, Lincoln, when Mr Wilkinson rushed up to him and blurted out his story. The officer took possession of the gun, and quickly made his way to the scene. The man had a fatal gunshot wound to his temple and was subsequently identified as Nathan Bagley.

A Coroner's Inquest was held the following day. After hearing evidence from Mr Wilkinson, and Constable Calvert, the Jury then heard from Ella. She said that, although Nathan was clearly sulking after his conversation with her father at the weekend, he had seemed all right in himself the previous evening. She added that, when Nathan produced two bullets she assumed they were not real, and it had never crossed her mind that he owned a gun and might harm himself.

The Coroner then read a letter to the Jury. The letter had been found in Nathan's jacket pocket and was addressed to Ella's parents saying, *"It is very hard for me to part with the one I love so much, and for whose love I would die. Mr Denton knew what wage I got and, if he did not want us to go together, why did he not stop us before I got so dead in love with her, and to love her so much? This is all through Mr Denton saying I cannot have her because I have no trade in my hands. So, if I cannot have her after 15 months of true love, I will die for her. It is hard to say goodbye, but it is for love's sake. I cannot have anyone else going off with her."*

The Jury returned a verdict of "Suicide whilst temporarily insane."

What happened next?

James Nathaniel Bagley was buried in plot D189 at St Swithin's Cemetery in Lincoln, on April 26th. He was 20 years old.

Ella remained single for many years but, at the age of 44, she married William Henry Haynes (a pattern maker) at St Andrew's Church, Lincoln, in 1921. The couple made their home at Hall Cottage, Chapel Lane, Heighington. Sadly, their marriage did not produce any children. She passed away in November 1942, aged 66, and is buried in plot M125 at Canwick Road New Cemetery.

Primary source; Newark Advertiser, April 30th, 1902

27: Rose Dale

1903 - Lincoln: Senselessly Shot

Rose Annie Gibson Dale was baptised at St Botolph's Church in Quarrington (near Sleaford) on July 24th, 1881. Records show that her parents were John (an agricultural labourer) and Louisa Dale and that she had four siblings. By 1901 the family had moved to nearby Sleaford and the census recorded her occupation as a pea packer. By 1903, Rose was working as a barmaid at the Lord Nelson Inn, in Lincoln. However, by this time she had stopped using the surname Dale, and preferred to be known as Rose Gibson.

During the evening of Thursday, April 2nd, 1903, two men, named Fred Pools and Charles Roper, were drinking in the bar at the Inn. Pools was the proud owner of a gun which he had recently purchased and he showed it to Roper. The gun was loaded with cartridges which contained dozens of pellets. Roper then asked if he could examine the gun more closely, and Pools passed it to him. Pools omitted to mention that it was loaded. In an act of inexplicable foolishness, Roper then rested the barrel on his forearm, and aimed it at group of people standing nearby.

Roper then saw Rose walking towards their table. He aimed the gun at her and said, "Look up Rose," and pulled the trigger. The gun went off and the pellets hit Rose's face from a distance of just a few yards. Rose screamed loudly, clutched her face, and fell to her knees. Roper was horrified to see what he had just done and kept muttering, "I didn't know it was loaded." Someone sent for Doctor Jenkinson.

The doctor rendered first aid at the inn and had Rose removed to his surgery where he could examine her more closely. He found that 14 small pellets had hit her face, and eight had hit her neck. By some miracle, none of the injuries were life-threatening, and Rose's vision was unaffected. Doctor Jenkinson skilfully removed the pellets from Rose's flesh and arranged for her to be taken to her parent's house in Sleaford to recuperate.

What happened next?

It seems that detectives accepted Roper's explanation that the shooting was accidental, as he was never charged in connection with the incident.

The author would like to be able to inform the reader that Rose made a full recovery and went on to have a full life, but the evidence is somewhat inconclusive. There are no records to show that she died, or married in the UK at any time between 1903 and 1990, and she does not appear in either the 1911 or 1921 census.

However, a lady called Rose Dale (born around 1882) was a passenger on a liner which sailed from Southampton to New York in 1912. Could this have been the same person?

Primary source; Lincolnshire Chronicle, April 3rd, 1903

28: Louisa North

Branston - 1905: A Forgiving Victim

Louisa was born at Branston, near Lincoln, on November 18th, 1886, to David and Sarah North. Her father was an agricultural labourer and the family lived in an isolated cottage in Branston Fen near to the bank of the River Witham

By 1903, Louisa had matured into a 17-year-old teenager who started to attract the attention of young lads from the village. However, she rejected these advances in favour of 28-year-old local man named Fred Goodacre, who had a limp on account of a spinal deformity since birth. The couple started courting, and became engaged at the beginning of 1905.

At 7pm on Saturday, September 23rd, 1905, Louisa and Fred walked over the bridge to the Anchor Inn at Bardney, and returned around 9pm. When they arrived at Louisa's home, Fred asked Louisa if she would stay out a while longer. Louisa agreed to this and the couple walked off towards a water course known as the "New Cut". Once there, Fred suggested that Louisa should leave her parents and come away with him to Tattershall. Louisa refused, but said she would reconsider after all of the potatoes had been harvested. At this point Fred placed his arm around Louisa's neck, threw her to the ground and started hacking at her neck with a razor. Louisa struggled valiantly and, despite receiving some nasty cuts, she managed to free herself and ran all the way home.

Louisa's father sent for help. Doctor Sidebotham found that the cuts to Louisa's neck had missed major blood vessels but she had some deep cuts to her hands. Meanwhile Police Sergeant Pacey took Fred into custody and charged him with attempted murder. However, when Fred appeared at the Lincolnshire Assizes on Friday, December 1st, the charge had been reduced to one of unlawful wounding. Fred pleaded Guilty and was sentenced to six months imprisonment.

What happened next?

It seems that Louisa forgave Fred, as the couple got married the following year. The 1911 census shows that they were living at Branston Fen, and had two young children. Fred sadly died from natural causes in 1933.

In 1936 Louisa married a farm labourer named Joseph Haw at Bardney. She went on to have a long life and passed away in 1978 aged 91.

Primary source; Boston Guardian, October 7th, 1905

29: Herbert Pickering
Lincoln 1906: A Drunken Wife-Beater

Herbert was born in Boston, in 1868, to a young unmarried woman named Betsy Pickering, and was raised by his grandmother Eliza who lived at 2 Pinfold Lane in the town. He trained to become a boot-maker and moved to Lincoln after 1891. On December 9th, 1893, he married 21-year-old Mary Ellen Townsend (always known as Polly) at St Michael on the Mount Church, Lincoln.

The couple rented a house at 3, Brummitt's Row (off St Martin's Street), where Mary soon discovered that whilst Herbert was perfectly well behaved when he was sober, he could be very nasty when he had been drinking. Mary left him on four occasions during the first 18 months but each time, Herbert begged her to come back to him, with promises that he would reform.

On May 13th, 1895, Herbert left the house leaving nothing but dry bread in the pantry. He returned several hours later, worse for drink, and demanded his dinner. Mary replied that without any money, she was unable to buy food. Herbert then struck Mary with a violent blow, and then kicked her in the ribs whilst she was lying on the ground. Mary left her husband and summonsed him to appear at court. The magistrates heard the case on May 15th, and found Herbert Guilty. He was fined £1 and Mary was granted a separation order. Somewhat predictably however, Herbert persuaded Mary to come back to him and the 1901 census shows the couple were living together at 185, High Street, Lincoln.

There were no further reports of trouble between the couple until 1906, by which time they were living at 4, Wesley Court (off Grantham Street). On July 19th, 1906, Herbert attacked Mary whilst drunk. He gave her a severe beating and threatened to kill her. Mary reported the matter to the police who brought him before the Magistrates on August 1st. They found the case proved and he was fined 10 shillings. Mary had had enough. She moved to live with a friend on Monks Road, and started working at The Plough Boy public house on Burton Road.

On Wednesday, August 15th, 1906, Herbert paid a visit to the Plough Boy and spoke with Mary. True to form, he pleaded with her to return to him but Mary said, "I will not, and I have given you my final answer." Herbert then said, "If you are still here tomorrow, I shall wait for you." Then as he started to leave, he turned and added, "I will do you one."

At 7:30am the next day, Mary was in the smoke-room at the Plough Boy. She was on her knees cleaning the iron legs of one of the tables, with her back to the door, when Herbert walked in. He was served by the landlady and sat down at one of the tables with a bottle of beer. After drinking it he said, "Well Polly my lass, I am going." Mary replied, "And a good job too!" At this point Herbert came up behind Mary, took hold of her hair and pulled her head backwards. With his other hand, he then placed a razor to Mary's throat and drew it swiftly across her windpipe. As luck would have it, Mary had instinctively brought her hand up to her throat to protect herself. The razor cut straight though Mary's glove. It inflicted a deep cut to her finger, but her neck was unharmed.

Herbert fled the scene but was arrested two days later. He was remanded in custody and appeared before Mr Justice Ridley, at the Lincoln City Assizes, on November 27th, 1906, charged with attempted murder. He pleaded Not Guilty. After hearing evidence from Mary and the landlady of the Plough Boy the Jury returned a verdict that Herbert Pickering was Guilty of a lesser charge of unlawfully wounding Mary. Herbert was imprisoned for nine months with hard labour.

What happened next?

Mary never went back to her husband and turned her back on Lincoln. By 1911 she was working as a live-in house keeper for a Methodist Minister in Louth. The 1921 census shows that she was then living at Holbeck in Leeds but details of her life beyond this point are inconclusive.

Herbert Pickering moved to Conisburgh, Yorkshire, after his release from prison, and resumed his work as a shoemaker. It appears that he learned his lesson and became a law-abiding citizen until his death in 1933 aged 65.

Primary source; Retford and Worksop Herald, December 4th, 1906

30: William Feary

Lincoln - 1906: A Mining Accident

Records from St Swithin's Church, Lincoln, show that William Henry Teesdale Feary was baptised on December 24th, 1882 and that he was the eldest of five children born to Thomas (a labourer) and Ann Feary. William spent his early childhood living at Fishermen's Court (off Waterside North) but, by 1889, the family had moved to 3, Williamson Square (off Bridge Street). After leaving school, William worked alongside his father as a bricklayer's labourer, but in 1903, father and son both started working at Greetwell Quarry, on the outskirts of the city.

Works at the quarry began in 1871 to extract ironstone which was used in the production of iron and steel. By the early 1900s the extensive workings covered a vast area and included (what is now) the Allenby Industrial Estate, the Deacon Road area and land to the east of Outer Circle Road. The various parts of the site were connected by horse-drawn tramways which took the rich ore to a main-line railway siding. Some of the mineral lay close to the surface and was quarried using open-cast mining methods, but much of it lay in rich seams below the surface, and was extracted by men digging tunnels (known as adits) into the ground.

On the morning of Wednesday, March 8th, 1906, William and Thomas were both mining ore in one of the adits. William, being the younger man, undertook the arduous task of loosening the rock using hand tools, whilst Thomas' role was to bring the ore to the tunnel entrance. At 11:30am Mr Aubrey Mackenzie, assistant manager, visited the entrance to the adit and spoke with Thomas to assure himself that everything was running smoothly. Thomas then disappeared into the gloom to continue his work.

At 11:35am Samuel Daft and Charles Martin, who were working in a nearby section of the quarry, heard groaning noises from the tunnel. They rushed to the entrance and found that a quantity of rock and earth had fallen from the roof of the tunnel onto the men. They immediately began removing the loose debris with their bare hands and soon found Thomas. He was still alive but his legs were trapped. Fearing a further collapse, they extricated him with the utmost caution, and he was taken directly to the County Hospital for treatment. Surgeons subsequently found it necessary to amputate part of his left foot.

The operation to reach William was much more difficult as he was entombed by rocks at the furthest part of the adit. Sadly, when rescuers eventually reached him, they found that life was extinct. His body was taken to the public mortuary where a post-mortem examination established that death was due to a broken neck.

William was 24 years of age, and was married with two young children. He was buried in plot C166 at St Swithin's Cemetery. Records show that William had made a will, but his estate was valued at less than £5.

What happened next?

Thomas Feary made a good recovery and went onto have a long life. He died at home, on Goldsmith Walk, in 1934 aged 79.

William's widow, Ann, struggled to cope on her own with two young children. However, in 1908 she married a labourer named Richard Bray who treated William's children as his own. The couple lived at 25, Rasen Lane, Lincon, and they had a son of their own in 1909.

Primary source: Lincolnshire Chronicle, March 9th, 1906

31: Frank Clawson

Lincoln - 1908: An Abominable Man

Frank Hollis Clawson was born in Lincoln in 1875 to William (a carpenter) and Amelia Clawson. He was one of 5 children and the family lived at 65, King Street, Lincoln. After leaving school he trained as a carpet fitter and moved to Rawtenstall in Lancashire, where he married 18-year-old Sarah Schofield in 1897. The couple had seven children together, but he deserted his wife in 1903. Sarah had him arrested twice for failing to support her, and he was imprisoned for a month on each occasion. In 1906 he had an affair with a 16-year-old girl in Stirling (Scotland) who became pregnant by him. The girl sadly died during childbirth. He moved back to Lincoln in 1908 where he worked as a boatman, and formed a relationship with Charlotte Elizabeth Dobbs.

Charlotte was born in Lincoln on April 27th, 1893, and was one of four children. Her parents were Thomas (a carter) and Charlotte Dobbs, and the family originally lived at 2, Orchard Houses, Orchard Street, Lincoln. By 1905 the family had moved to 32, Grantham Street. Tragically their mother died unexpectedly in 1906, leaving Thomas to raise the children on his own.

When Charlotte met Clawson in 1908 she was only 14 years old, but that did not stop them becoming intimate within a few weeks of their meeting. In the first instance, Clawson took Charlotte to the cabin on his vessel which was moored on the river, and she subsequently accompanied him on several boat trips where they lived as man and wife. However, by May 1908, Clawson had moved into 32, Grantham Street, where he shared a bed with Charlotte in a room directly next to the one occupied by her father.

By the beginning of November, 1908, Charlotte was heavily pregnant and people started to talk. One of them informed the police. Clawson was arrested on November 4th and charged with "Unlawfully and carnally knowing a certain girl, Charlotte Elizabeth Dobbs, being above the age of 13, and under the age of 16 years." Charlotte's father was also arrested and charged with knowingly allowing Clawson to commit the offence on his premises.

The pair appeared before Mr Justice Luft on November 8th, 1908. Thomas Dobbs pleaded Guilty, but Clawson claimed that he thought Charlotte was at least 17 when they first started sleeping together. The Jury did not believe him and found him Guilty. In passing sentence, the Judge addressed Clawson and said, "You do not care how much misery you have caused to one young woman after another, because you are determined to live in an abominable way." Clawson was imprisoned for 15 months with hard labour. He then turned to Thomas Dobbs and said, "It was your duty as a father to protect this young girl, and to prevent her from coming into contact with wicked people, but you have actually connived at it, and allowed it to go on in your own house." He then jailed Thomas Dobbs for nine months with hard labour.

What happened next?

Charlotte gave birth to a healthy baby girl, named Alice, on January 7th, 1909, and married a man named George William Foley (sometimes given as Folley) later that year. However, as soon as Clawson was released from prison, she abandoned her husband and started cohabiting with Clawson at 27, Chaplin Street, Lincoln.

Charlotte Foley and Frank Clawson continued living at the same address until their respective deaths. Clawson died in 1954 aged 78, and was buried in plot J178 at Canwick Road New Cemetery, Lincoln. Charlotte passed away in 1970, aged 77, and was buried in the same grave.

Charlotte's daughter, Alice, married Stanley Roulinson in 1931 and their only child was born in 1938. Sadly, Alice was widowed in 1945 when Stanley lost his life in a road accident on Nettleham Road, Lincoln. Alice never remarried and passed away in Lincoln in 1994 aged 85. She was laid to rest in Newport Cemetery.

Primary source; Retford and Worksop Herald, November 17th, 1908

Research note:

The name of the 16-year-old girl in Stirling was not mentioned during the trial. It is not known if her baby survived.

32: Sarah Parrish

Lincoln - 1908: Sent for the Doctor but...

Sarah Frances Burton (always known as Fanny) was born at Winterton, near Scunthorpe, in 1858, to Joseph (a plumber) and Mildred Burton. She was one of four children and the family lived at 15, Low Street.

On September 30th, 1879, Fanny married 25-year-old William Joseph Parrish at All Saints Church in Winterton. The couple then made their home in Old Basford, near Nottingham, where Joseph worked as a joiner. Children soon followed and, by 1891, the couple had four daughters. For reasons which have not been documented, in 1897, Fanny abandoned her family and she went to live with her recently-widowed mother in Winterton.

In 1902, Fanny then relocated to Lincoln where she formed a relationship with a labourer named John Lidgett of 9, Gadsby's Court (Sincil Street), in Lincoln. John was a teetotaller and had not touched a drop for several years, but this did not discourage Fanny from drinking to excess on a regular basis. Between 1902 and 1908, she appeared in court at least four times, charged with drunken behaviour. Indeed, such was her reputation within the city, that gangs of boys would sometimes follow her down the street taunting her with insults such as, "You old-born drunk," or, "You drunken old sot."

By 1908, Fanny's dissolute lifestyle was starting to take its toll. John had found it difficult to get work, they were behind with the rent, and most of their possessions had been pawned by Fanny to buy drink.

On the morning of Sunday, July 11th, 1908, Fanny complained of having a sore throat. She asked for a drink of water, but she found it so difficult to swallow that John had to trickle it down her throat using a spoon. He sent a neighbour to fetch a doctor, but when Mrs Aisthorpe returned, she informed him that the doctor would not attend unless he was paid half-a-crown in advance. John sat at Fanny's bedside until 1:30am the following morning when Fanny suddenly raised herself and grabbed John's arm saying, "Good-bye, I am going." Fanny then lost consciousness, and died shortly afterwards.

A Coroner's Inquest was held at the Sessions House on Tuesday morning, where John furnished details of Fanny's excessive drinking and the last hours of her life. The Coroner then pressed him for more details about why a doctor did not attend and John replied, "I only had half-a-crown. What was I to do without anything to eat?" The Coroner then said, "Oh, I see, you were so afraid of starving yourself, that you would not spend the money on a doctor?" John replied, "Yes, sir." The Coroner then questioned Mrs Aisthorpe in an attempt to establish which doctor had refused to attend. Mrs Aisthorpe replied, "When I was on my way to the doctor, I was told that no doctor would come for less than half-a-crown, so I never went for one".

Doctor Rees-Jones testified that he had conducted an autopsy and that the cause of death was heart failure. The Jury returned a verdict of, "Death from natural causes, accelerated by excessive drinking."

John Lidgett was censured by the Coroner for failing to summon medical assistance promptly.

What happened next?

Fanny was 50 years old and is buried in St Swithin's Cemetery.

Records relating to John Lidgett are inconclusive.

Primary source: Sleaford Gazette, July 11th, 1908

Footnote:

Half-a-crown was a coin which represented two shillings and sixpence. It is roughly equivalent to £19 in today's money.

33: William Williamson

Bracebridge - 1909: Tried his best

William was born at Bracebridge, near Lincoln, in 1896, to Richard (a machinist) and Rose Williamson. The 1901 census shows that he was one of five children living at 21, Albany Terrace but, by 1909, the family had moved to 17, Saville Street, Bracebridge.

Monday, January 27th, 1909 was a bitterly cold day and the water courses around Lincoln had frozen solid. William (then aged 12) and his younger brother, John, finished their day of study at Bracebridge School and made their way to the Plough Inn on Newark Road. They then went onto the bank of the River Witham and clambered onto the ice.

The two lads had great fun sliding along and soon reached a point near to Hampton's Field where the catch-drain feeds into the river. John was slightly ahead at this point and he fell through thin ice into the water below. William shouted for help and, as he rushed to assist John, the ice gave way beneath him. William grabbed hold of John, who could not swim, and tried to keep his head above water. William struggled valiantly for several minutes, but eventually his strength gave way. He had to release his grip and John disappeared below the surface. A lad named Charles Boucher, who had heard the cries for help, rushed to the bank and succeeded in dragging William to safety. John's body was recovered by police officers using drag lines later that evening.

A Coroner's Inquest was held the following day into the circumstances of the incident. The Jury returned a verdict of, "Accidental death," and commended Charles Boucher for his bravery.

John Henry Williamson was 10 years old and was laid to rest at All Saints Church, Bracebridge, on January 30th, 1909.

What happened next?

At the outbreak of The Great War, William Williamson joined the 1/4th (Territorial) Battalion of the Lincolnshire Regiment. After initial training at Grantham, Belper and Luton they mobilised for war and landed at Le Havre in March 1915. The Regiment was engaged in various actions on the Western Front and, by October 1915, they had joined the 1/5th Regiment in the trenches near Hohenzollern in northern France, where the German forces held a heavily fortified stronghold known as the Hohenzollern Redoubt.

Shortly after dawn on Wednesday, October 13th, a two hour artillery barrage rained upon the German positions, after which William and his colleagues advanced across no-man's land in four lines. A bloody battle ensued which resulted in the capture of the Hohenzollern Redoubt, but a great cost. William was one of 169 men from the 1/4th Lincolnshire Regiment to be killed in the battle, and a further 228 were wounded or taken prisoner. The 1/5th Lincolns suffered 483 casualties, including 188 men killed.

William was 19 years old and has no known grave. He is commemorated on the large war memorial on Lincoln High Street, and the smaller memorial in Bracebridge.

Primary sources:
Lincolnshire Echo, January 28th, 1909
Lincolnshire Echo, October 14th, 2020

34: Daisy Williams

Lincoln - 1909: A Sordid Case

Daisy was born in Lincoln, in 1893, to Herbert (a slater) and Nellie Williams. She was one of five children and by 1909 the family were living at 1, Kirton Square (off Waterside South), in Lincoln. Neighbours noticed men coming and going to the house on a very regular basis and reported their concerns to the police.

On Saturday, February 13th, 1909, Constables Croft and Clarke were instructed to observe the house from 9pm onwards. The officers watched as Daisy Williams and her mother took turns at accosting men in the street, and then taking them into the house. At one point, Daisy and her mother were both "entertaining" men within the house at the same time, so the officers approached silently and listened at the window. The officers were able to hear explicit conversations which indicated that sexual activity was taking place. Their records showed that, over the course of three hours that they were watching, Nellie and Daisy took 8 different men into the house.

The two women appeared before Lincoln Magistrates on Wednesday, February 17th, 1909, charged with "keeping a disorderly house" (see footnote). Nellie and Daisy were both found Guilty. In passing sentence, the Chairman addressed Nellie and said, "We can scarcely believe there could ever have been a more abominable case of prostitution. We commit you to two months imprisonment with hard labour." He then addressed Daisy by saying, "We think you have been under the pernicious influence of your mother, but you are 18 years of age, and should have known better. You will be fined 40 shillings, or if you fail to pay within 14 days, then you will serve one month in prison with hard labour." Daisy paid the fine.

What happened next?

Daisy married Alfred Middleton in 1913 and they had a son in 1920. Sadly, her husband died a few months before the baby was born. Daisy subsequently worked as a housekeeper for different families and managed to raise her son single-handedly. During the last years of her life she lived at 63, Outer Circle Drive, Lincoln, where she passed away in February 1954, aged 62 years. Daisy was buried in Newport Cemetery.

The 1911 census shows that Daisy's parents were still living together, as lodgers, at 1 Danesgate, Lincoln. Herbert Williams died in June, 1913, aged 43. He was buried in plot F146 at St Swithin's Cemetery. In later life Nellie Williams lived at 14, Michaelgate, Lincoln, where she passed away in November, 1934. She was buried in the same plot as her husband, at St Swithin's Cemetery.

Primary source; Retford and Worksop Herald, February 23rd, 1909

Footnote: A disorderly house is described as "A brothel or a place staging performances or exhibitions that tend to corrupt, deprave, or outrage common decency".

35: Gertrude Makins

Lincoln - 1910: Beaten with a Poker

Eva Gertrude Makins (always known as Gertrude) was born in the small hamlet of Brampton, some 10 miles west of Lincoln, in 1896. Her parents, John and Kate, rented a cottage with a small plot of land and could best be described as subsistence farmers. Life was difficult, and, by 1903, the family had moved to 9, Spencer Street, Lincoln.

By 1906 the family had six children, but tragedy struck when Kate died unexpectedly the following year. Kate's funeral took place at Torksey on April 27th, 1907, after which the family moved to 4, Latham Place, (off Rasen Lane), Lincoln

By the winter of 1909 the two eldest daughters had both left home, leaving 13-year-old Gertrude to look after her three younger siblings. John decided he would advertise for a housekeeper to cook and help look after the children. There was only one applicant, and a young widow named Emily Outram was appointed.

By March the following year the family came to the notice of the NSPCC. Inspector Welling visited the home on March 3rd, and was shocked by what he found. The only furniture downstairs was a single chair and a wooden box which was used as a table. The children had to sit on the floor, or stand when eating. The conditions upstairs were even worse as all of the occupants of the house shared one mattress on the floor. The children were dirty, scantily-dressed, and infested with lice. John was warned that he needed to make drastic improvements.

The inspector returned to the house on March 12th. There was no improvement at all, so he called Doctor Winter to examine the children. He found the younger children were under-nourished, blue with cold, and covered with scratches and bite marks from vermin. Then, whilst the doctor was examining Gertrude, she informed him that two days previously her father had punched her in the mouth, kicked her about her body and told her to go and drown herself.

The NSPCC prosecuted John for ill-treating Gertrude and for neglecting the others. He appeared at the Lincoln City Police Court on March 24th. Magistrates first heard from Inspector Welling and Doctor Winter about what they had seen and heard. Two police officers then testified that Gertrude had approached them on March 10th, complaining about being punched by her father. Her face was swollen and her lips were bleeding. They went to the house and spoke with John Makins. He completely denied the allegation.

Emily Outram testified that she had done what she could to look after the children, but John had not paid her a single penny since she arrived, and he had never given her any money to buy food or clothes for them. She then added that, to prevent the children from starving, she had sold or pawned all of her own possessions.

Gertrude testified that she was now living at St Swithin's Children's Home. She described how her father had punched and kicked her on the 10th of March, and went on to say she had been subjected to physical abuse for a long period of time, and that, at Christmas he had beaten her with a poker.

In mitigation, John Makins said that Gertrude had been living a very bad life for more than three years and had been spreading rumours that he had been indecently interfering with her. He went on to say, "She has seen more than any woman of 25, and knows more." One of the Magistrates then said, "Well, are you surprised when you all sleep in the same bed?"

The Magistrates found the case proved and sentenced John Makins to three months imprisonment with hard labour.

What happened next?

With no mother, and their father in prison, Gertrude and her younger siblings were placed in the workhouse together, but were then subsequently sent their separate ways.

Gertrude was placed in a Doctor Barnardo's Home and sent to Canada under their Child Migrant Scheme. She arrived in Nova Scotia in March 1911, and was sent to work in Ontario. She married Harold Leonard Cross (originally from Boston, Lincolnshire) in Ontario in 1921 and gave birth to a daughter named Loris in July, 1922. Tragically, Loris passed away when she was just a few weeks old. Details of Gertrude's life beyond this point. are inconclusive.

Records show that Gertrude's younger sister Caroline was also a child migrant and arrived in Quebec in 1912.

Gertrude's younger brother John remained in Lincoln. He married Cissy Hollis in 1923 and they had a daughter together in 1929. John died in Lincoln in 1982 and is buried in Newport Cemetery.

Their youngest brother Benjamin was informally adopted by the Millson family from Ferry Road, Bardney. The 1939 Register shows that he was still a single man and was living with the same family. He died in 1944.

Their housekeeper, Emily Outram, eventually found happiness when she married William Edward Smith (a farmer) at Bassingham in 1918. In later life the couple lived on Bridge Street, Deeping St James. She was widowed in 1942 and passed away in 1947, aged 81 years.

Primary source; Retford and Worksop Herald, March 29th, 1910

36: Martha Stothard

Lincoln - 1910: A Family Affair

Martha was born in Derby on October 17th, 1894, and was one of six children whose parents were William (a factory labourer) and Sarah Stothard (sometimes given as Stathard). When she was a small child, the family moved to 19, Fairfax Street, Bracebridge, Lincoln.

On May 16th, 1908, Martha's older sister, Mary, married Walter Hardwick at St Swithin's Church in Lincoln. The couple made their home at Grange de Lings (3 miles north of Lincoln) where Walter worked as a groom. By the summer of 1910, Mary was the mother of two very young children and she asked Walter if she could have a domestic servant to help her around the house. Walter was reluctant to spend money needlessly and suggested they should ask 15-year-old Martha to come and live with them. Martha accepted, and moved to the house on August 26th, 1910. She proved herself to be very helpful around the house and provided much needed companionship for Mary.

On Wednesday, October 5th, 1910, Martha agreed to look after the children for the afternoon whilst Mary went into Lincoln to meet friends. It was implied that Mary would not be returning until teatime, but she unexpectedly came home shortly after 3pm. The house was quiet, as the children were both having an afternoon nap, but Mary then heard the sound of giggling coming from Martha's room. She entered, and found her husband and Martha in bed together. Mary instructed them both to get dressed and ordered Walter out of the house. Later that evening, Martha confessed that her relationship with Water had been consensual, and that it had started the day after she moved to Grange de Lings.

After consulting with her parents, Mary decided she would make an example of Walter, and made a formal complaint to the

Lindsey Police. He was arrested on August 12th, and charged with "Carnally knowing a certain girl, being over the age of 13, and under the age of 16 years". Walter Hardwick appeared before Mr Justice Bucknill at the Lincolnshire Assizes, on October 31st, and pleaded Guilty. He was sentenced to 15 months imprisonment with hard labour.

What happened next?

The 1911 census shows that whilst Walter was in prison, Mary and her two children went to live with her maternal grandparents at Harby (eight miles west of Lincoln). After Walter was released in 1912, the couple got back together, and moved to the village of Coleby (six miles south of Lincoln). Tragically, Mary passed away two years later. She was just 27 years old and was buried in the village graveyard on October 7th, 1914.

A year after Mary's death Walter married Lucy Mary Heslam. The couple had two children of their own, and the 1921 census shows that both of Mary's children were still living in the same household. Walter was taken ill shortly before Christmas later that year, and became very depressed. On January 2nd, 1922, he made his way to the railway line between Coleby and Harmston, and lay down on the track in front of an oncoming train. He was killed instantly. He was 35 years old and was buried at Coleby two days later.

What happened to Martha?

The 1911 census shows that Martha Stothard had moved back to Bracebridge and was living with her sister, Elizabeth, at 12 Fairfax Street. She married Fred Houtby (a foundry labourer) in 1918. The couple had at least three children and lived at 105, Holly Street, Bracebridge. She passed away in 1973, aged 79.

What happened to Mary's children?

Ivy Hardwick married Fred Bagley in 1934. They established their home on High Street, Harmston, and had two children. She was widowed when Fred passed away in 1971 but went on to have a very long life. She passed away in 2001 aged 93.

Records relating to the younger child, Charles Walter Hardwick, are inconclusive.

Primary sources:
Retford and Worksop Herald, October 18th, 1910
Illustrated Police News, January 12th, 1922

37: Zilpah Cheseldine

North Hykeham - 1911: A Painful Tragedy

Records from St Michael's Church, in Waddington, record that Zilpah (sometimes given as Zelpha, or Zilpeh) was baptised on December 21st, 1884, and that her parents were Moses (an agricultural labourer) and Caroline Staples. She was one of five children, and the family lived in a farm cottage, in Harod's Yard, in the village. The 1901 census shows that she was then working as a domestic servant for the Brocklesby family (farmers) at Carlton le Moorland. When she was 19, she met George William Cheseldine, a bricklayer's labourer from 105, Newland Street West, Lincoln. The couple were married in Lincoln in 1910, and rented a house at 5, Nelson's Cottages, Newland, Lincoln.

Details of the first 5 years of their marriage have not been documented, but 1910 should have given them cause to celebrate when Zilpah discovered she was pregnant. Unfortunately, Zilpah's pregnancy was very troublesome; she suffered from nausea during the early stages and from excruciating pain in her lower back during the last few months. During the same period, George was diagnosed with consumption (tuberculosis) and was admitted to a sanatorium for treatment. Zilpah gave birth to a healthy baby girl, named Elsie, during the second week of December, 1910, but the delivery was a very traumatic affair and Zilpah was, "Very much weakened and melancholic" afterwards. In desperation, Zilpah returned to Waddington where her mother helped to look after both of them.

Over the following weeks, Zilpah found it difficult to sleep and complained of constant pains in her head. A doctor was summoned, and he left Zilpah with some tonic to restore her health. By the end of January however, she was very tearful and told her mother she wanted, "To do away with myself, and the baby, as the trouble is more than I can bear."

At 10am, on Monday, January 30th, 1911, Zilpah informed her mother that she was going for a walk with Elsie, and intimated that she would be going to Harmston to see her sister. However, instead of taking the road which led towards Grantham, she walked down Station Road and then took the back lane towards North Hykeham where she lingered on the bridge over the River Witham.

At 11am the same morning, a farmer who was crossing the bridge, found a woman's blue coat, a skirt, a hat and a baby's shawl, neatly arranged, on the river bank near the bridge. He also saw a set of footprints leading to the water's edge, and reported his discovery to Police Sergeant Bradshaw at North Hykeham. Sergeant Bradshaw and Constable Hinch made their way to the scene and dragged the river for several hours, but had to abandon their efforts when it began to get dark. Numerous police officers, under the direction of Superintendent Jarvill, resumed the search at first light. Elsie's body was found amongst reeds near the Plough Inn at Bracebridge around 10am, and Zilpah's body was recovered from 4 feet of water, a mile upstream from the Plough Inn, about an hour later.

A Coroner's Inquest was held at the Plough Inn the following day. After hearing evidence about the state of Zilpah's mental health, the Coroner informed the Jury that they had a difficult decision to make by saying, "If the mother drowned herself and the child then, strictly speaking, she would have taken her own life and murdered her own child." After careful deliberation, the Jury returned the verdict that Zilpah had, "Committed suicide whilst temporarily insane," and that baby Elsie had been, "Found drowned'.

What happened next?

Zilpah, aged 26 years, and Elsie, aged 7 weeks, were buried in the same grave at St Michael's Church, Waddington, on February 3rd, 1911.

George Cheseldine eventually recovered from consumption. In 1920 he married Ethel Odling, but the relationship was childless. The couple subsequently moved to the Lincolnshire coast where George passed away in 1938, aged 55. He was laid to rest at St Mary's Church in Winthorpe.

Primary source: Retford and Worksop Herald, February 7th, 1911

38: Walter Reeve

Lincoln - 1912: A Runaway Horse

Walter George Reeve was born in Clenchwarton, near Kings Lynn, in 1877. He was one of six children whose parents were William (an engine driver) and Jane Reeve. Sadly, his father passed away when Walter was just seven years old, leaving the family in very difficult circumstances. His mother, who was originally from Metheringham, decided to move the family to Lincolnshire to be closer to her relatives. They rented a house at 2, Hungate, Lincoln, and his mother made ends meet by taking in other people's washing and by working as a charwoman.

After leaving school, Walter gained employment as an unskilled labourer, and married Emily Bunn at St Martin's Church on January 7th, 1899. They rented a house at 35, Holland's Row (off Depot Street, Lincoln), and, by 1911, they had six children under the age of 11 years.

George Wright was a 35-year-old machinist who lived just around the corner from the Reeve family at 11, Carholme Road, Lincoln, with his wife Alice and two young children. Shortly after lunch on Sunday, June 23rd, 1912, George went to his stable and hitched his horse to a trap. He then brought it to the street in front of his house to collect his family. The horse was a bit frisky so two men held its head, whilst George helped Alice and the baby into their seats. At that moment the animal shook its head violently, causing the two men to lose their grip, and it broke into a canter.

Meanwhile, Walter had just turned the corner from Depot Street onto Carholme Road, when he saw the horse coming towards him at a considerable pace. Instead of stepping out of the way, he stood directly in front of the speeding animal, with outstretched arms, and shouted, "Woah!" Unfortunately, the horse did not slow down, or change direction. Walter tried to leap out of the way at the last moment, but it caught his shoulder, spun him around, and the trap's wheel then passed directly over his trunk. The horse continued towards the Fossdyke where it slackened its pace, and a man named Dunn brought it under control.

Alice and the baby were completely unharmed, but Walter was writhing in the street in great agony. Doctor Lambert was summoned and attended immediately. It was obvious to him that some of Walter's ribs had been broken so he instructed that Walter should be removed to the County Hospital in the ambulance van. Tragically, Walter's condition deteriorated and he passed away later that afternoon.

What happened next?

News of the event caused a sensation in the city, and the Mayor started a subscription to help raise funds to pay for Walter's funeral and to provide some relief for his widow and family. The appeal raised £83 (worth over £12,000 today) and Walter was buried in plot G462 at Canwick Road New Cemetery. He was 35 years old.

Shortly after the event, Chief Constable Coleman submitted a report to the Carnegie Heroes Trust Fund (see footnote). Walter's name was inscribed upon their Roll of Honour, and they generously agreed to provide ongoing support to the family. Emily Reeve was awarded 10 shillings per week for herself, and 10 shillings and 6 pence for each child until they reached the age of 14.

In later life, Emily moved to Yorkshire. She never remarried and passed away in Bradford in 1952, aged 73.

Primary source: Nottingham Evening Post, August 31st, 1912

Footnote:

The Carnegie Heroes Trust Fund was established in 1908 by a wealthy American philanthropist, Andrew Carnegie, who donated over $350 million to various charities before his death. The fund still exists and, to date, it has given over $44 million in grants, scholarship aid, death benefits, and ongoing assistance.

39: Rose Annie Coles

Lincoln - 1913: A Dreadful Fall

Rose was born in Lincoln in 1888 to John (a boilermaker) and Rose Norton. She was one of two girls, and the family lived at 8, Abbey Place (off Montague Street), Lincoln. By 1900, the family had moved to Croft Street, where Rose's mother sadly passed away on March 5th, 1900. Unfortunately, their father was unable to cope with the two girls on his own. Help was at hand however, and they were informally adopted by Joseph (their mother's brother) and Hannah Daft, who lived at 6, Nottingham Terrace, Lincoln.

History has not recorded what Rose did after she left school but, shortly after her 21st birthday, she married Harry Orman Coles, who worked as a caretaker at Central Hall. The 1911 census shows that the couple were both living with the Daft family, but when Rose discovered she was pregnant the following year, they moved to a home of their own at 20, Spa Buildings (Rosemary Lane), Lincoln. Their son, Harry N Coles, was born in February 1913.

Central Hall was a large building on St Swithin's Square, Lincoln. When it first opened, in 1902, it served as a meeting hall for the temperance movement but, by 1904, it was also used as an entertainment venue, for plays, pantomimes and film shows. The auditorium, which could seat over 1,000 people, was bathed in natural light during the day on account of it having several large skylights. This however, posed a problem whenever films were shown, as there were no blinds, or shutters to darken the room. Consequently, whenever a film was due to be shown, Harry was required to enter the false roof space above the skylights to place thick layers of newspaper over the glass.

On the morning of Monday, April 7th, 1913, Harry was feeling slightly unwell, so Rose volunteered to accompany him to the hall to help remove the newspapers. The couple ascended the steep stairs which gave access to the roof space, and Harry started removing the covers. However, the act of bending over made Harry feel dizzy so, as a precaution, Rose held his hand to steady him. Harry had almost completed the task when he stood on a nail which was protruding from a piece of wood. He was still holding Rose's hand at this point, and his sudden movement caused Rose to fall headfirst through the glass.

Rose fell 60 feet and landed awkwardly across the back of one of the plush chairs in the auditorium below. Harry rushed to her side expecting the worst, but found she was still alive, and raised the alarm. Doctor Serres attended and rendered first aid, before sending for an ambulance to take her to the County Hospital. Upon arrival, Doctor Lyons found that Rose had complex fractures to her left arm and left leg, along with cuts to her face. Sadly, Rose never regained consciousness, and passed away that afternoon.

A Coroner's Inquest was held the following day. Harry wept constantly as he related the sequence of events. A reporter, who was present, recorded that Harry, "Broke down after giving his evidence, and had to be assisted from the chair." After hearing medical evidence, the Jury then heard from Police Sergeant Milner who had examined the scene of the tragedy. He explained that the false roof consisted of several oblong panes of glass which were surrounded by footboards which were only 18 inches (45cm) wide. He went on to say that, in his opinion, "Anyone who happened to stumble, would not have the slightest chance." He also suggested that the glass ought to have been protected by strong wire mesh.

The next witness was Mr T Starke, Secretary of the Lincoln Temperance Society. He testified that, "Coles is a good fellow, who never complained of having been ill, and his wife was a happy little woman." He expressed his deep regret at what had happened, and added that the Society would take immediate measures to prevent a recurrence. The Jury returned a verdict of,

"Accidental death" and recommend that guard rails should be placed around the skylights.

What happened next?

Rose was buried in plot 209, at St Swithin's Cemetery. She was 25 years old.

What happened to her baby?

Harry N Coles was informally adopted by his paternal grandparents in Deeping St James. Sadly, he succumbed to illness and passed away in November 1918, aged five.

What happened to Harry Coles?

After his son's death, Harry tried to make a new start in life. He married Madeline Fenton in 1920 and she gave him a son, named Phillip, in June 1922. He also started a new career, and qualified as a Registered Mental Nurse at Mapperley Hospital, Nottingham, on May 16th, 1924. Tragically, he died unexpectedly in September, 1930. The Hospital Board awarded Madeline an "in-service gratuity" of £195, but details of her life (and that of their son Phillip) beyond this point, are inconclusive.

Primary source: Lincolnshire Echo, April 10th, 1913

Footnotes:

Rose and her sister were obviously deeply upset at losing their mother, but whilst Rose somehow managed to cope, her older sister Ethel had a nervous breakdown, and was admitted to the "Bracebridge Asylum" on February 26th, 1901. Records show that she was discharged as "Recovered" on August 7th, 1902. Her recovery was however, short-lived, and the "Lunacy Register" shows that she was re-admitted on July 20th, 1904. On December 10th, 1939, she was transferred to Caistor Hospital (formerly Caister Union Workhouse), where she passed away in 1947, aged 63.

Central Hall was destroyed by fire on March 6th, 1944. The ruins were demolished in 1960 and an eight storey building was constructed on the site. It was initially used as an office block by Ruston Gas Turbines (later renamed European Gas Turbines), but has now been remodelled as a luxury apartment block.

40: George Meggitt

Lincoln - 1914: A Dangerous Game

George was born in Lincoln on October 18th, 1908, to David (a tinsmith) and Fanny Meggitt. He was one of three children and, by 1914, the family were living above David's business premises at 50, Broadgate, Lincoln. The building was three storeys high and George slept in the front bedroom on the top floor which overlooked the street below.

Around 8:45am on Saturday, March 7th, 1914, George asked if he could help the maid (Elizabeth Crow) to make-up the beds. This was something which he had done many times before and his mother readily agreed. Elizabeth and George then ascended the stairs to the top floor. It seems that, at this point, George had second thoughts about helping Elizabeth, because he went straight into his own room to play, whilst she worked in the back room. After a few minutes Elizabeth thought she heard an adult's voice shouting from the direction of the front room and went to investigate. As she entered the room, she noticed that the sash window was wide open and caught a glimpse of George's feet disappearing from view. She rushed downstairs to tell Fanny what she had seen.

Meanwhile, Arthur Morley, (aged 10), of 8, Croft Street, was walking along St Rumbold's Street. As he approached the junction with Broadgate, he glanced at the buildings directly opposite and saw a young boy looking out of the window on the top floor. The window was wide open. Moments later he heard a man shout an alarm and, as he turned around, he saw the boy hurtling downwards towards the footpath.

Fanny Meggitt's heart was pounding as she ventured out of the house. She saw George crumpled in the gutter with blood coming from one of his ears, then watched as Constable Hinton gently lifted George in his arms. George was still breathing so the officer carried the boy into the house and sent for a doctor. Doctor Powell came quickly, but George stopped breathing shortly after the doctor arrived.

A Coroner's Inquest was held two days later. The court heard evidence that the latch on the sash window was very loose, and that it was possible to raise the lower portion of the window with minimal effort. The Jury also heard that, when George's limp body was lifted from the gutter, a number of marbles were found directly beneath him. In summing up, the Coroner thought it probable that George had been playing with his marbles on the window sill and that he had overbalanced to retrieve one which had dropped onto the ledge outside. The Jury returned a unanimous verdict of, "Accidental death," and expressed their deepest sympathy to his family.

George Wilson Meggitt was only five years old. He was laid to rest in plot E392, at Canwick Road New Cemetery, Lincoln.

Primary source, Retford & Worksop Herald, March 17th, 1914

41: James Upton

France - 1915: Conspicuous Gallantry

James Whitbread Upton was born in Victoria Street, Lincoln in 1888. His mother was Hannah Upton and his father was James Whitbread. The relationship between his parents was not conventional. Both were married - but not to each other, as they were both living apart from their respective partners. Their relationship fizzled-out some five years after James was born. He was educated at St Peter at Gowts School, after which he served an apprenticeship at Ruston, Proctor & Company. He then moved to Nottingham to work at Rigley's wagon works in Bulwell.

In 1906 James decided to join the Army and enlisted in the Sherwood Foresters. He served in Ireland and India but, in November 1914, the Battalion was sent to the Western Front in France. On 9th May 1915 James was involved in heavy fighting at Rouges Bancs during the Battle of Auber's Ridge, where he displayed conspicuous gallantry. His citation reads:

"For the whole of the day Corporal Upton displayed the greatest courage in rescuing the wounded whilst exposed to very heavy rifle and artillery fire, going close to the enemy's parapet regardless of his own personal safety. One wounded man was killed by a shell whilst this non-commissioned officer was carrying him. When Corporal Upton was not actually carrying the wounded, he was engaged in bandaging and dressing various cases in front of our parapet exposed to the enemy's fire."

In July, 1915, James was granted a period of extended leave during which he was presented with the Victoria Cross by King George V at Windsor Castle. He also took this opportunity to marry his childhood sweetheart, Mary Jane Chambers, at St Faith's Church in Lincoln. James survived the war, and the couple went on to have three sons.

What happened next?

By 1929, James and Mary had divorced. The reasons for the marriage breakdown have not been documented. James moved to Kingsbury in North London and became the proprietor of a nightclub. He joined the Home Guard during WW2 and reached the rank of Major. He died in July 1949 and was cremated at Golders Green Crematorium.

Primary source: Lincolnshire Echo, July 1st, 1915

42: Linnell Family

Lincoln - 1915: Brothers in Arms

Percy Linnell was born in Lincoln in 1896, and was one of 12 children born to George (a moulder) and Kate Linnell of 33, Mill Lane, Lincoln. He was particularly close to his brother Clarence, and they were both pupils at St Botolph's School, where they had almost perfect attendance records. As young men, they both completed apprenticeships at Messrs Robey's works, and both played football competitively in their spare time. Percy was the captain of Lincoln Rovers, and Clarence played for the St Peter's United team.

When war was declared against Germany in 1914, Percy, Clarence and their older brother Ralph enlisted in the 4th Lincolnshire Regiment. All three brothers were assigned to "A" Company under the command of Captain Meaburn Staniland. After a period of training near Luton, they were shipped to France and landed at Le Havre on March 1st, 1915. They then marched to Ypres in Belgium and linked up with the British Expeditionary Force who were defending the town against German forces. Their Regiment was sent to the front line near Hooge, about 3 miles east of Ypres, where they were under constant attack from three sides throughout June and July. By the third week in July, the front line had moved back and forth several times as each side gained a few hundred yards of territory, but then lost it in the next counter-attack.

Tuesday, 27th of July, 1915, began as a quiet day in the trenches around Hooge. The sound of military action further along the line could clearly be heard, but the lull in fighting in their sector provided some welcome relief for the brothers. Around 1:45pm, Percy and Clarence were engaged in idle conversation in one of the trenches when, out of the blue, a shrapnel shell burst directly above them. Ralph witnessed the incident from his own position nearby, and rushed to the scene where he found Percy and Clarence's mutilated bodies. Ralph had the painful task of writing home to his parents. In his letter, he explained that his brothers had felt no pain, as they had died instantly. He went on to say that, later that night, he attended their funeral where the chaplain, "Read the burial service over them, and it was carried out just the same as if it had been in England. The chaplain gave me every comfort, and prayed that you would both be comforted."

By the time the letter from Ralph arrived, George and Kate Linnell had already received a telegram from Captain Staniland in which he expressed deepest sympathy from himself, and from everyone in the Company. He spoke of the two brothers as being, "Excellent soldiers, and great favourites in their platoon." He ended by saying, "I hope the knowledge that they died doing their duty may be of some help to you in bearing your great loss."

What happened next?

Ralph Linnell married Sarah Robinson in 1916 whilst on home leave and he survived the conflict. After the war, the couple lived at 94, Vernon Street where they had eight children. Ralph passed away in 1967, aged 75.

Captain Meaburn Staniland, who was originally from Boston, was not so lucky. Just two days after Percy and Clarence were killed, he was observing enemy positions over the parapet, when he was shot by a sniper. He was buried at Dranouter Cemetery near Ypres.

Percy Linnell was 19 years old and is buried in plot 11M14 at Sanctuary Wood Cemetery near Zillebeke, Ypres. Clarence Linnell was 21 years old and was interred in the adjoining grave. Both brothers are commemorated on the large war memorial in Lincoln City Centre.

Primary source: Retford and Worksop Herald, August 10th, 1915

Research notes:

At one time, George and Kate Linnell had five sons fighting in The Great War. The two which have not been mentioned thus far are George and Herbert.

George Henry Linnell, born in 1877, was one of the older siblings. He joined the Royal Navy in 1892 and served on, HMS Impregnable, and the Royal Yacht, Victoria and Albert. He married Alice Macklin at Portsmouth in 1906 and they had two children. When war was declared, George was transferred to HMS Agincourt (a dreadnaught battleship) which took part in the Battle of Jutland. He continued serving after the war and was transferred back to the Royal Yacht. He left the service in June 1921. The 1939 Register shows the couple were living on Winchester Road, Portsmouth, and that George was working as a gateman at a local factory. George passed away in Portsmouth in 1948, aged 71.

Harold Linnell, born 1898, was one of the younger siblings. He joined the Lincolnshire Regiment in 1915, and was undergoing training near Luton at the time of his brothers' deaths. He survived the conflict and married Florence Inman at St Botolph's Church, Lincoln, in 1922. The couple had two children. The 1939 Register shows they were living at 7, Westwick Drive, Lincoln, and that he was working as a press-hand at an engineering works in the city. Harold passed away in 1979, aged 80.

43: William Palmer
Waddington - 1917: First Solo Flight

William was born in Kingston-upon-Thames on October 23rd, 1896. He was the only child of William (a merchant) and Jane Palmer. He was a brilliant student and gained prizes for mathematics and chemistry at Finsbury Technical College. However, upon reaching military age, he suspended his studies and joined the London Regiment (Artists Rifles) in October 1915. After a period of training, he joined the first line battalion of his Regiment at St Omer in France, where he served with distinction.

Having made an application for transfer to the Royal Flying Corps (RFC), William was then sent to the school of Aeronautics in Oxford, where he passed his exams with flying colours. He was given a commission, and attended a short practical course at a civilian flying school, before being posted to the No. 47 Training Squadron of the RFC at Waddington, near Lincoln. During the first two weeks, he made several flights whilst accompanied by an experienced instructor who assessed him as being ready to make his first solo flight.

At 8am, on Saturday, September 15th, 1917, William climbed into a Maurice Farman "Shorthorn" biplane. He went through his pre-flight checks, then trundled across the airfield before climbing to a height of 100 feet. He then started a slow turn to the south but, as he did so, his left wing started drooping in an alarming fashion. The aircraft then stalled, plummeted to the ground near the perimeter of the airfield, and burst into flames.

Ground crew rushed to the scene and managed to pull William from the burning wreckage. He was taken to the Red Cross hut in the first instance, but was then transferred to the 4th Northern Military Hospital in Lincoln. Upon arrival he was assessed by Lieutenant Colonel W. Brook of the Royal Army Medical Corps.

William's head and face had been badly burned and his right leg and thigh "were burnt to a cinder". William sadly succumbed to his injuries and he passed away a few hours later. A Coroner's Inquest heard that the cause of death was shock due to severe burns and the Jury returned a verdict of, "Accidental death."

What happened next?

William was buried with full military honours on Wednesday, September 19th, 1917, at Ham (near Richmond, Surrey). Six colleagues from RFC Waddington bore their fellow officer to his resting place in the churchyard, and three volleys were fired over his grave, followed by the sounding of the Last Post. He was 20 years old, and had never married.

Primary sources:
Lincolnshire Echo, September 17th, 1917
Electrical Engineer's World War 1 Roll of Honour, 1924

Footnote:

The 4th Northern Military Hospital was based at (what is now) Lincoln Christ Hospital School, on Wragby Road, Lincoln. Temporary accommodation was constructed on the playing fields to provide 41 beds for officers and 1126 for other ranks. During the course of The Great War some 45,000 injured men received treatment for their injuries at the facility.

44: Mary Routledge

Lincoln - 1920: A Fatal Fire

Mary was the eldest of nine children born to John and Sophia Garner and was baptised at All Saints Church, Stamford, on July 4th, 1847. The 1851 census shows that the family were living in Oakham, where her father worked as a wheelwright. By 1861 however, her parents had moved to Lincoln, and Mary was living with her paternal grandparents on Scotgate, Stamford.

Mary went into service after leaving school, and by 1870 she was working for the family of a Wesleyan Minister named Ralph Spoor, who lived in Driffield, in the East Riding of Yorkshire. She married George Routledge later that year and the couple rented some rooms in Driffield. However, by April 1871, George had lost his job as a labourer at Thacker's Linseed Cake Mill. The couple then moved to Linthorpe, a suburb of Middlesborough, where Mary gave birth to her first child, Jane, during the autumn of 1872.

By 1877, the family had moved to 14, Stanley Street, in the booming industrial city of Lincoln, where George tried to earn his living as an insurance agent. However, by 1891, the family were living on Steep Hill, Lincoln, and George had established himself as a newsagent. Mary helped by delivering newspapers, over a wide area, on a daily basis.

By 1900, Mary had given George six children. None of their offspring had married, and they all lived in a two-bedroomed terraced house at 10, Spital Street. It is not known how they celebrated Christmas that year, but tragedy struck two days later when Jane, aged 18, passed away. Her death was due to natural causes, and she was buried in plot F4 at Newport Cemetery.

By 1911, the family had moved to 105, Winn Street, Lincoln. The business had devolved to their son Ernest, and he was running it successfully from new premises on St Mary's Street. George however, was still involved, and he could be found selling newspapers from a stand near the Stonebow.

By 1920, the couple were living at 51, Steep Hill, Lincoln, and both were in poor health. Mary was, by now, an invalid who regularly experienced seizures, and George, described as "a cripple", did his best to nurse her. During the afternoon of Thursday, January 22nd, 1920, neighbours noticed smoke coming from a window at 51, Steep Hill, and forced entry. Upon entering Mary's bedroom, they found her laying prone across the fire, with her night clothes alight. The fire brigade was summoned, They quickly rescued Mary, and extinguished the blaze. Mary had terrible burn injuries to her head and body, but she was still alive, and was rushed to the County Hospital. Sadly, Mary passed away the following morning. It was thought the tragedy occurred as a result Mary of getting out of bed, having a seizure, and losing her balance.

What happened Next?

Mary, who was 72 years old, was buried at Newport Cemetery, Lincoln and shares a grave with her daughter Jane. Her husband George, passed away in 1925, aged 75.

Primary source: Nottingham Journal, January 23rd, 1920

45: Frederick Vickers

Lincoln - 1922: Rescued Two Men

Frederick was born in Dunholme, Lincoln, on October 17th, 1874. He was the youngest of four children whose parents were William (a labourer) and Maria Vickers. The family moved to the Newport area of Lincoln when Frederick was an infant and, after leaving school, he served an apprenticeship as a boiler maker for Messrs Clayton and Shuttleworth.

Frederick subsequently gained employment at Marshall's Engineering works in Gainsborough where he met Annie Gertrude Bland. The couple got married in 1901, and made their home at 14, Marlborough Street, Gainsborough. Their two daughters, Elsie and Kathleen were both born in the town. In 1916, the family then moved to 44, Harris Road, Lincoln, on account of Frederick getting a new job as maintenance engineer at the Lincoln Corporation Power Station at Stamp End.

During the afternoon of Tuesday, September 5th, 1922, Frederick was working in the boiler house at the plant. His colleagues, Charles Pendlebury and Edward Shaw, were undertaking some routine maintenance during which it was necessary for one of them to enter the boiler-drum to examine an internal pipe. Charles carefully removed the access panel, squeezed through the opening (measuring 11 inches by 15 inches), and entered the drum. He collapsed almost immediately. This was witnessed by Edward who thought Charles had simply fainted, and he wriggled through the opening to rescue him. Within seconds, Edward started to feel light-headed, and shouted for assistance.

Frederick heard the shout and quickly realised that his two colleagues had probably been overcome by toxic fumes. He wisely decided against using the same method of entry. Instead, he unbolted an inspection cover at the opposite end of the boiler, knowing that this would allow some of the noxious gas to escape. When he finally entered the drum, he found that both men were now completely unconscious. After great exertion, he succeeded in dragging Charles and Edward through the hatch. Although feeling sightly dizzy himself, Frederick performed artificial respiration, and both of his colleagues regained consciousness. All three men were taken to the County Hospital for further treatment, and they all made a full recovery.

Frederick's bravery was widely recognised; The Mayor of Lincoln presented him with a silver medal on behalf of the Royal Humane Society and Lord Liverpool presented him with "A certificate on vellum", and a £10 reward on behalf of the Carnegie Hero Trust Fund.

What happened to the men he rescued?

Charles Pendelbury was a married man with four young children. He lived for another 48 years before passing away in 1970, aged 75.

Edward Shaw married Gracie Elvidge in 1927. They did not have any children, but Edward lived for another 40 years before passing away in Battersea in 1962, aged 76.

What happened to Frederick's family?

Frederick's life was touched with tragedy when his daughter, Kathleen, died unexpectedly from an illness in 1930. She was 20 years old and was buried in plot T282 at Canwick Road New Cemetery, Lincoln.

In later life Frederick and Annie moved to 6, Simon's Green, in the Boultham area of Lincoln. Frederick died in April, 1946, aged 71, and Annie passed away in 1953, aged 73. They were both buried in the same grave as Kathleen.

Their other daughter, Elsie, married Wilfrid Lill (an insurance agent) in Grantham in 1939. The couple made their home at 2,

Ashley Avenue, Grantham. It is believed the marriage was childless. In later life the couple moved to Beeston, Nottinghamshire where Elsie passed away in 1955, aged 50.

Primary source: Lincolnshire Echo, January 2nd, 1923

Footnote:

Tragically, despite modern Health and Safety Regulations and specialist training, working in confined spaces still accounts for around 15 deaths each year in the U.K.

46: George Baker

Lincoln - 1922: A Fit of Depression

William George Baker (always known as George) was born at Chippenham, Wiltshire, in 1884. He was one of 10 children born to Henry (an engineer) and Susan Baker. After leaving school, he trained as an engineer at Nestle's Condensed Milk Factory in the town. However, in his early twenties, he relocated to Lincoln. He took lodgings at 15 Sibthorpe Street, and gained employment in one of the nearby engineering works.

George remained single until he was 26 years old, when he met Clara Fry, who was also from the Chippenham area. The couple found they had a lot in common, and got married at St Peter at Gowt's Church, Lincoln, on December 22nd, 1910. They rented a small terraced house at 21, Norris Street, and had a son in 1912.

Unlike many of his peers, George did not volunteer to join Kitchener's Army when war was declared against Germany in 1914, but he contributed to the war effort through his skilled work in Lincoln's munitions factories. Shortly after the war ended however, military contracts dried-up and many engineering companies, claiming they faced insolvency, tried to modify the long-standing agreements they had with the engineering unions around issues such as: rates of pay, the length of the working week, and overtime.

Protracted negotiations over many months ended in deadlock and, during the spring of 1922, engineering employers in England announced a "lockout' where the factories would close until unions agreed to their terms. George was a member of the Amalgamated Engineering Union and received strike-pay during the dispute. This however, was considerably less than he earned during the course of normal employment, and, as his family began to experience financial difficulties, George's mental health started to deteriorate. The lockout finally ended, after 13 weeks, when unions agreed to revised terms proposed by the employers on Tuesday, June 20th, 1922, and thousands of engineering workers, including George, returned to their factories the following day to sign their new contracts.

Just 18 days later, at 2:30am on Sunday, July 9th, 1922, Clara Baker awoke from her sleep to find George sitting on the edge of the bed, holding his head in his hands. Clara asked her husband what was troubling him. George made no reply but immediately jumped to his feet. He then ran down the stairs, opened the front door, and ran into the street wearing nothing but his nightshirt. Clara followed him down the stairs a few seconds later, and saw him running at full speed towards Scorer Street. When George reached the bridge over the Sincil Drain, he climbed onto the parapet and dived, head-first, into the murky water 20 feet below. Rescuers went into the water some 30 minutes later, but found his head was, "Firmly wedged in the mud, with his feet in the perpendicular position."

An inquest into George's death was held the following day. The Jury heard that George was burdened with debts which had accrued during the lockout, and that he had complained about his new "piecework" contract, where he was paid on the basis of the work he produced, rather than the hours he worked. He found it was physically impossible to earn a living-wage and had a nervous breakdown. The Jury returned a verdict that George had, "Died from suffocation during a fit of depression."

What happened next?

George was buried in plot Y108 at Canwick Road New Cemetery. He was 37 years old.

The 1939 Register shows that Clara was still living at 21, Norris Street, with their son, and she was making ends meet by working as a charwoman. Clara never remarried. In later life, she lived on Keddington Avenue, Lincoln, where she passed away in

1969, aged 82. She shares her grave with George at Canwick Road New Cemetery.

Their son, who was also called William George Baker, married Charlotte Johnson at St Luke's Church, North Carlton in May, 1940. He reached the age of 91, before passing away in May, 2003.

Primary source: Sheffield Daily Telegraph, July 11th, 1922

47: Thomas Martin

Lincoln - 1923: A Faulty Rope

Thomas was born in the small village of Holywell, near Melton Mowbray, in 1883, to Matthew (a wheelwright) and Mary Martin. The 1891 census shows that the family had moved to Heydour (near Sleaford), and that Thomas was the eldest of six children.

After leaving school, Thomas took lodgings with the Boyce family at 42, Canwick Road, Lincoln, and worked as a baker for Mr Boyce's family business. He subsequently served an apprenticeship at Messrs. Robey and Co Works, and married local girl, Elsie Dickinson, in 1914. By 1922, the couple were living at 39, Ellison Street, Bracebridge and had four children (including a set of twins) under the age of 6.

On Friday, December 22nd, 1922, Thomas went to work at 7am as normal. His job, as a core maker, involved making complex moulds (or cores) out of compacted sand; molten metal was subsequently poured into the moulds to make components for Robey's machines. During the course of the morning Thomas and his colleagues made dozens of cores which were then loaded onto large trucks. The loaded trucks were then pushed along rails into a massive drying oven.

Once the drying process had finished, Thomas and his colleagues started pushing the trucks out of the drying oven onto the factory floor. However, when they tried to push the last truck, it stubbornly refused to move. The workshop foreman, John Parkinson, attached a heavy rope to the truck. He then assembled a team of twelve men, including Thomas, and gave instructions to grab the rope and start pulling. Under the combined effort of a dozen men, the truck moved a fraction of an inch. Mr Parkinson then gave the instruction, "All together now, heave!" The rope snapped and all of the men fell to the ground. They got back to their feet quickly but Thomas complained, "I have cracked my head on that other truck." Thomas completed his shift and returned to work the next day.

The family enjoyed Christmas Day together but Thomas was very subdued, and went to bed early that night. He was clearly unwell the following morning, and complained of pains in his head. Elsie sent for Doctor Sherrard, who suspected that Thomas was suffering from concussion, and sent him to hospital. Thomas showed marginal improvement over the next three weeks but there was very little they could do for him. It was then agreed that he should be sent back home to convalesce under the care of Doctor Sherrard.

Thomas never recovered and passed away at his home on Sunday, December 16th, 1923, almost a full year after he was originally injured. An inquest was held at the Sessions House the following day where evidence of identification was given by Elsie. Mr Parkinson and two other employees then described the circumstances leading up to Thomas banging his head.

The Jury then heard from Mr C J Patterson, Inspector of Factories who said he had investigated the accident shortly after it happened. He estimated that the truck and its load weighed five tons and the rope used to pull it was more than adequate for the task. However, when he examined the point where it had broken, he discovered a flaw which would not have been visible prior to it breaking. The Jury returned a verdict of, "Accidental death."

What happened next?

Thomas was laid to rest at Canwick Road New Cemetery on December 19th, 1923. He was 39 years old. Elsie raised the four children single-handedly before marrying Thomas King (a library clerk) in 1935. Elsie was widowed in 1973, and passed away in January 1976 aged 81.

Primary source; Stamford Mercury, December 21st, 1923

48: Ernest Rosling

Lincoln - 1924: A Fatal Miscalculation

Ernest was born in Lincoln in 1904, to Harry (a painter) and Florence Rosling. The 1911 census shows that the family lived at 60, Baggholme Road, Lincoln, and that Ernest was one of eight children. When he was a teenager, the family moved to 223, Wragby Road, in the north of the city. After leaving school, Ernest gained employment as a furnaceman at Claytons Wagons Ltd (a subsidiary of Clayton and Shuttleworth Ltd), at the Abbey Works, Spa Road, Lincoln. In addition to his job at the Works, Ernest was a (part-time) soldier in the 4th Battalion, Lincolnshire Regiment (Territorial Force). He was a keen musician and played the clarinet in the Regimental Band.

In January 1924, Ernest was redeployed to the workshop to assist with the manufacture of Austin flywheels. The process involved the use of a 2,500kg drop forge hammer to "stamp" the metal moulding into the desired shape. The process started when the hammer was dropped twice onto the moulding, from a height of 8 feet. At this point, Ernest was required to use a long metal bar to prise the moulding from its die, so that another worker could get hold of it with a large pair of tongs. The moulding was then turned over, replaced in the die, and given another 8 blows. Ernest would then use the bar to lever the moulding out of the die and the process would repeat itself.

The first few hours of Thursday, September 25th, 1924, passed without incident, but shortly after 11:30am Ernest made a mistake which would cost him his life. Maybe he was momentarily distracted but, instead of waiting for the hammer to fall eight times, he inserted the bar as the hammer was in the process of dropping for its eighth time. The hammer struck the bar smartly, causing it to fly lengthways into his abdomen.

Ernest was rushed to the County Hospital where he was diagnosed with having major internal abdominal injuries. Doctor Wells-Cole decided to operate immediately. The operation revealed that there was a large tear, some six inches long, in the wall of his stomach, and he had a ventral hernia (see footnote). Ernest survived the operation but he sadly passed away the following day.

A Coroner's Inquest was held on Saturday. The Jury returned a verdict of, "Death by misadventure," and attached no blame to anyone.

What happened next?

Ernest was buried, with full military honours, at Newport Cemetery on Tuesday, September 30th. He was just 20 years old, and had never married.

Primary source; Retford & Worksop Herald, September 30th, 1924

Footnote:

A ventral hernia occurs when parts of the intestine, or other tissue, protrude through a weakness in the abdominal wall. In the 1920s the surgical repair of a ventral hernia was considered to be a major procedure. In the present day, the operation is usually performed by way of laparoscopy (minimally-invasive keyhole surgery)

49: George Wilson-Dutton
Lincoln - 1924: Pram in the Fossdyke

George was born in Leamington Spa, Warwickshire, in 1886 to George (a labourer) and Elizabeth Wilson-Dutton. After leaving school he entered service as a footman but later obtained employment as a drilling machinist at one of the factories in Lincoln. He married Olive Cowling in the Gainsborough district during the first three months of 1910. The couple rented a house at 35, John Street, Lincoln, and their son was born in September the same year.

After the outbreak of war with Germany, George and his family were relocated to a purpose-built machine gun factory at Burton-on-Trent and the family remained there until the cease of hostilities. After the war, they returned to Lincoln and George started a wholesale confectionary business, along with a sweet shop known as "Cosy Corner" at 1, Fosse Bank, Lincoln.

Lizzie Ashcroft lived just around the corner on Staunton Street, Lincoln, and was the mother of two young children named Sydney (aged three) and Irene (aged eight months). On the afternoon of Tuesday, February 12th, 1924, she wrapped both children in warm clothes and placed them in their perambulator. She walked into the city centre to buy some groceries. On the return journey, Lizzie stopped at Cosy Corner to purchase some treats for her husband. She left the pram outside the shop, with the hood up to protect the children from the elements, but omitted to set the brake.

George had just starting serving Lizzie when he heard loud cries of alarm from outside. George rushed out of the shop and was just in time to see the perambulator being blown down a slight incline towards the Fossdyke. It then toppled over a low wall, entered the water, and floated towards the deepest part of the canal. George dived in fully-clothed, rescued baby Irene, and brought her to the bank. When Lizzie then informed him that there was another child, George dived in for a second time, and brought Sidney to safety.

George was hailed as a hero and was presented with a certificate from the Royal Humane Society by the Mayor of Lincoln on Thursday, May 1st, 1924.

What happened next?

Sadly, George's business had been floundering for some time, and he was declared bankrupt in October, 1925. He subsequently moved to Epsom in Surrey where he died in 1932 aged 46. His wife, Olive, passed away in 1935, aged 45.

What happened to the children that he rescued?

Sydney Ashcroft married Kathleen Wright at Halifax in 1941 and they had at least one child. He died in Cornwall in 1992, aged 71.

Irene Ashcroft married Ronald Parker in Lincoln in 1943, and their daughter was born in Gainsborough the following year. Details of Irene's life beyond this point are inconclusive.

Primary source: Lincolnshire Echo, May 1st, 1924

50: Rhoda Carr

Washingborough - 1925: A Loaded Shotgun

Rhoda was born in Worksop on October 24th, 1914, and was one of three children born to Walter (an agricultural labourer) and Hannah Carr. When she was a small child, the family moved to Lincolnshire after her father obtained a new job as farm foreman at Top Farm, Washingborough. The job came with an impressive stone-built house, set on a rise, on the outskirts of the village. Rhoda was described as a "sweet-faced girl, who was rather tall for her age." She attended the Heighington Girls' School, where her engaging smile won her many friends.

The afternoon of Saturday, April 25th, 1925, was a beautiful sunny day. Rhoda's mother had decided to go into Lincoln to do some shopping, and her father was busy in the yard tending to his horses, leaving Rhoda at the kitchen table doing her homework.

At 3:15pm, Rhoda's brother, Herbert (aged 14), came into the kitchen. He did not speak, but he became intrigued when he saw his father's double-barrelled shotgun in the corner of the kitchen. He picked up the gun and, at that instant, it went off. Rhoda dropped to the floor, motionless, with a grievous injury to her neck. Herbert ran outside shouting, "Come Dad, Come dad. I have shot my sister." Walter rushed into the house and saw Rhoda lying on the rug with a gaping hole in her neck. He galloped to Heighington to fetch Doctor Pomeroy, but there was absolutely nothing the doctor could do to revive her.

A Coroner's Inquest was held at the farm two days later. Walter Carr testified that he had purchased the gun about two months ago. It was a normal double-barrelled shotgun but the trigger mechanism was very sensitive. He had last used the gun on Friday, May 1st, to shoot vermin. He then cleaned the gun and left it propped-up against the wall in the corner of the kitchen. He went on to say that he always left the gun unloaded and, for safety reasons, the ammunition was kept on the top shelf in the pantry. The Coroner then asked, "How did the cartridge get into the gun?" Walter replied, "I don't know Sir."

Herbert was then called to give an account of the events, and described how he picked up the gun to examine it. He admitted that he had touched the trigger, but his touch was very light, and the gun seemed to go off on its own.

In summing up, the Coroner, said it was a very serious matter to leave a loaded gun unattended. He made the point that the cartridge could not have got into the weapon by itself. He suggested that Walter must have forgotten to take the cartridge out of the gun after cleaning it.

The Jury retired and returned a verdict of "Death by Misadventure". The Coroner informed Herbert that he was very lucky not to have been committed to the County Assizes on a charge of manslaughter, and lectured him sternly about playing with guns.

What happened next?

Members of the Jury were much affected by the tragedy and they all donated their juror's fee to the family to help with the cost of the funeral. Rhoda, aged 10, was laid to rest in the graveyard at St John the Evangelist Church, Washingborough, on Wednesday, April 29th.

What happened to Rhoda's family?

After leaving school, Herbert Carr completed an apprenticeship and then worked for the Central Electricity Board as a linesman. He married Cora Luft in Bradford in 1935, and they had three children. He died in Nottingham in 1987, aged 77.

The 1939 Register shows that Rhoda's parents were living on Middle Street, Dunston, where her father worked on a pig farm. After retiring, the couple moved to 10, Almond Avenue,

Heighington. Walter passed away in 1965, aged 85. His wife, Hannah died in 1968, aged 82.

Primary source: Retford and Worksop Herald, May 5th, 1925

51: Margaret Cordey

Lincoln - 1926: The Coal Gas Tragedy

Margret was born in Lincoln on October 15th, 1925, to Frederick (a pensions revenue officer) and Lily Cordey. The family lived at 73, Addison Drive, Lincoln, and Margaret was their fourth child. Lily's pregnancy was very problematic and the delivery was described as being "difficult and protracted." Although baby Margaret was strong and healthy, Lily suffered from an acute form of anaemia which left her in a very weak condition. Lily found it difficult to sleep, and she struggled to cope with the daily routine of looking after the children. Frederick engaged a local girl to help Lily with the children during the day, and he slept in the spare room at night so as not to disturb her.

At 7:30pm on Saturday, February 13th, 1926, Frederick left the house to visit his parents. The older children had been put to bed, and Lily was left in the sitting room nursing the baby. Frederick returned at 10:15pm and found the house in complete darkness, apart from a candle on the window sill, just inside the door. He found a note next to the candle which read, "The hot water bottle is in your bed. Have gone to bed very tired, so don't disturb us. Good-night." Frederick lit another candle and went upstairs where, most unusually, he found Lily's bedroom door to be locked. He knocked and Lily replied, "Don't disturb us. We are very tired, and want a good night's sleep."

There was something about Lily's response which didn't seem quite right, so he sought the advice of Mrs King who lived next door. She agreed that Lily's behaviour was very unusual and accompanied Frederick when he knocked on Lily's bedroom door for the second time. Frederick then persuaded his wife to open the door.

As soon as he entered the room, Frederick detected a faint smell of coal gas (see footnote). He had a lighted candle in his hand and there was no explosion, but the smell was very noticeable. Frederick opened the bedroom window to ventilate the room and looked for a match to ignite the gas lighting in the room. Once the room was illuminated, Frederick saw that Lily had gone back to bed and was cradling Margaret in her arms. Instinctively, Frederick placed his hand on Margaret's forehead and found she was very cold. He asked, "What's the matter with the baby?" Lily replied, "It had a convulsion, and I gave it a mustard bath (see footnote). I believe it is dead". Frederick left Margaret and their baby in the care of Mrs King, whilst he went to fetch a doctor. Doctor Edwin Winter arrived at the house shortly after 11pm. He examined Margaret and quickly came to the conclusion that she had been dead for some time, and there was nothing he could do to revive her.

At this point, Frederick sent for a family friend named Mary Inkley from 27, Carlyle Walk. Mrs Inkley was a trained nurse, and she volunteered to sit with Lily overnight and the following day. Lily held Margaret's body close to her bosom all night, and tearfully carried Margaret from room-to-room the following morning. Around 10am, Mrs Inkley heard the sound of a cork popping in the scullery and went to investigate. Lily had a bottle of Lysol (see footnote) in her hand and put it to her lips. Mrs Inkley snatched the bottle out of her hand, and then noticed an empty cup on the shelf. The cup smelled of Lysol, and Lily admitted she had consumed a full cup of the liquid. Mrs Inkley mixed a large quantity of salt with some water and urged Lily to drink it. The mixture had the desired effect, and Lily vomited. An ambulance was summoned and Lily was taken to hospital.

A Coroner's Inquest was opened the following day, but was then adjourned on account of Lily being too poorly to attend. The Inquest resumed on Monday, March 16th and the Jury heard that, "Lily's health is such, that she may never recover." The Coroner decided the Inquest should go ahead without Lily's testimony. The Jury then heard from Doctor Winter who reported that he had conducted an autopsy upon Margaret's body. There were no marks about her body to suggest foul-play and the colour of her internal organs indicated that she had died from coal gas poisoning. He went on to say that Margaret had an enlarged thymus gland (see footnote) and this could lead to her being poisoned by the slightest trace of coal gas.

The Jury then heard from Frederick, who said the family had moved into 73, Addison Drive, in 1922. The house was not equipped with electricity and relied upon coal gas for cooking and illumination. On several occasions, Frederick had detected a faint smell of gas and asked the Corporation's Gas Department to investigate. They had attended, conducted tests, and made various modifications to the pipe work and fittings.

The next witness was George Twist, an inspector from the Corporation's Gas Department. He testified that he had recently attended 73, Addison Drive, along with Detective Inspector Skelson who was acting as an independent witness. He tested all the gas pipes, and fittings, and found them to be in perfect working order.

In summing up, the Coroner said he could not see any evidence which suggested that Mrs Cordey had caused the child's death. After protracted deliberation, the Jury found that, "The child met her death by coal gas poisoning, without sufficient evidence to show how such poisoning occurred." An open verdict was recorded.

Lily subsequently made a good recovery and, upon being discharged from hospital on Monday 12th April, 1926, she was charged with the crime of attempting to commit suicide. The court was in a merciful mood, and when they heard that Lily's mental health was still very fragile, they discharged her on condition that she voluntarily entered a mental hospital for treatment.

What happened next?

Sadly, the strain of Margaret's death took its toll on the relationship between Frederick and Lily. The 1939 register shows that she was living apart from her husband at 38, Central

Gardens, Merton, London. She went on to have a very long life and passed away in Merton in 1966 aged 80.

Frederick remained in Lincoln and lived at 163, Monks Road until his death in 1950, aged 72.

What happened to their children?

Their eldest child, Douglas, was born on December 1st, 1918. He was a very weak child and sadly passed away when he was just six hours old.

Their second child, Richard, was born in 1919. He became an analytical chemist and married Dorothy Stocker in 1948. Tragically, Richard passed away in December 1949 just a few months before their only child was born. He was only 30 years old.

Their third child, Francis, was born in 1922. The 1939 Register shows that he was working as a grocer's clerk in Merton, but details of his life beyond this point are inconclusive.

Primary source: Retford & Worksop Herald, February 23rd, 1926

Footnotes:

Mustard baths are a traditional remedy in England. It is fundamentally a mixture of water with mustard powder. Other ingredients, such as baking powder or essential oils were sometimes added. It was used for the treatment of colds, stress, fatigue, achy muscles, fever and congestion. Mustard has been known to stimulate the sweat glands, opening the pores and helping the body rid itself of toxins.

Lysol is a disinfectant which was invented in Germany in the 19th century to combat cholera. In the 1920s it was marketed in the UK as a feminine hygiene product. It contained a phenol-compound called Cresol, which is corrosive and highly toxic.

The thymus gland is in the chest, just above the heart. The thymus makes white blood cells called T lymphocytes (more commonly known as T cells). These are an important part of the body's immune system, which helps to fight infection.

Coal gas was made by heating coal in the absence of air and was widely used for lighting, cooking and heating. Its use was discontinued following the discovery of large quantities of natural gas in the North Sea in the late 1960s.

52: Ethel Maude Garner
1927 - Lincoln: Strangled her baby

Ethel was born in Lincoln on September 17th, 1904, to Herbert (a wheelwright) and Lucy Garner. She was one of four children and the family lived at 7, Moor Street, in the city's west end.

In 1919, Herbert Garner obtained a position as caretaker for Doctor Godfrey Lowe at 5, Cornhill, in Lincoln City Centre, and the family were allowed to live rent-free in rooms above his surgery. Ethel also started working for the doctor as an attendant, but she was a bright girl and was subsequently appointed as his book-keeper.

On Saturday, May 21st, 1927, Ethel worked as usual until shortly after 6pm. She then went upstairs and told her mother she had a pain in her side, and that she felt really unwell. Lucy Garner helped Ethel get into bed and said, "If you need me, just call me." Ethel replied, "That's all-right mum. You go to bed."

About 1am, Lucy heard Ethel calling for her and went to her room. She found Ethel standing next to her bed in a pool of blood. Ethel said, "Look mum," then fainted in her mother's arms. Lucy sent her husband to telephone for Doctor Charlotte Wilson, who lived nearby (see footnote). She came quickly but, when she saw how much blood Ethel had lost, the doctor sent her straight to the County Hospital.

Senior House Surgeon, Dr Durden-Smith, examined Ethel upon arrival at the hospital. She was barely conscious, her pulse was very weak, and she was haemorrhaging significant quantities of blood from between her legs. It was obvious to him that the girl had recently given birth to a full-term baby, but Ethel was unable (or unwilling) to say what had happened to it. The doctor gave priority to the patient lying before him and skilfully saved her life. He subsequently reported his suspicions about the birth to the City of Lincoln Police.

Police Officer Joseph Taylor had certain responsibilities, which included executing Warrants issued by the Court, and acting as Coroner's Officer to help investigate suspicious, or unexplained deaths. At 2pm the following day, he went to 5, Cornhill, and asked Herbert Garner if he might be allowed to check Ethel's room. Upon entering, he saw spots of blood on the floor near to the wardrobe and found the bottom drawer was locked. With permission, he broke the drawer open, and found the body of a full-grown male baby wrapped in a grey blanket. The child had a lady's stocking wrapped, and tied tightly, around its neck. The baby was taken to the mortuary where an autopsy established that the baby had breathed after he was born, and that death was due to asphyxia.

Ethel was eventually discharged from hospital on Thursday, 7th of July, and was brought before the City Magistrates later the same day charged with infanticide (see footnote). She was committed for trial at the next Assizes and released on bail.

Ethel appeared before Mr Justice Swift, at the Lincoln Assizes, on October 31st, 1927, where she was represented by Mr Lyons KC. Ethel initially pleaded Not Guilty to the charge of infanticide, but Mr Lyons indicated that Ethel would be prepared to plead Guilty to child concealment. At this point the Judge interjected by saying that, in his view, the evidence clearly supported the charge of infanticide and advised Mr Lyons that his client should plead Guilty. He then added, that he thought this was a very sad case, and he was inclined to be very lenient. Ethel then changed her plea to one of Guilty and expressed sincere remorse for what had happened. In passing sentence, the Judge started off by pointing out the gravity of what had happened but, before he could complete his sentence, Ethel collapsed and had to be removed from the court room. After a few moments, Ethel returned to court, and heard Mr Justice Swift announce that she would be bound over to keep the peace. Ethel walked away as a free woman.

What happened next?

The 1939 register shows that Ethel was living with her parents at 42, Moorland Way, and that she was employed as a shopkeeper.

In later life, Ethel moved to 27, St Andrews Gardens, Lincoln. She passed away in 1967, aged 63 years. Ethel had never married and it is not thought that she had any other children.

Primary source; Retford and Worksop Herald, November 8th, 1927

Footnotes:

Under English law, infanticide is both an offence in its own right and a partial defence to the charge of murder. Only a biological mother who kills her own child within 12 months of the birth can be charged with infanticide or rely on it as a defence. The death can be by either act or omission.

The author conducted some research to establish why Ethel's father telephoned for Doctor Charlotte Wilson, rather than calling for Doctor Godfrey Lowe. Records show that, although Doctor Lowe's surgery was at 5, Cornhill, he lived some distance away at 2, Curle Avenue in the north of the city. Records relating to Doctor Wilson are rather vague but newspaper accounts imply that she worked at the same practice.

53: Frank Jackson

Riseholme - 1927: A Furious Bull

Frank was born in Lincoln on September 15th, 1873 to John (a boilermaker) and Mary Jackson of 4, China Place (off Sincil Street), Lincoln. At the time of his birth, Frank was the youngest of three children, but over the following years, his parents would have nine more. Whilst he was still a small child, the family moved to 39, Coultham Street (see footnote).

After leaving school, Frank worked as a labourer in several of the local factories. He continued to live on Coultham Street with his parents until he was in his mid-twenties, and then spent the next three decades living under the same roof as his married sister, Jennie Herrick, in the Stamp End area of the city. By 1927, Frank was in his early fifties. He still lived with his sister in Lincoln, but travelled by bicycle to work as an agricultural labourer in the adjoining countryside.

On Tuesday, May 31st, 1927, Frank was engaged by a farmer, named Russon, to move a bull and a heifer from Grange Farm, Riseholme, to a field in North Carlton. The bull was a powerfully-built animal, but had a ring through its nose as a means of making it easier to handle. A length of rope was attached to the nose-ring, and Frank was given the job of walking with the bull. A man named John Francis, was put in charge of the heifer. The two men, along with the animals, left Grange Farm around 4:30pm, and set off down the track (now known as St George's Lane). However, when they reached Riseholme Road, the heifer broke loose with Mr Francis in hot pursuit.

At 4:45pm, an old woman, named Emily Oakes, was removing washing from her clothes line, when she heard an unusual sound coming from the direction of the road. She went to investigate and saw Frank, curled-up on the ground, being gored by a furious bull. She shouted for her husband who came at once. Without a thought for his own safety, 73-year-old Thomas Oakes distracted the bull by hitting it with a stick. He then took hold of the rope, pulled the bull away from Frank, and tied it to a tree. Mrs Oakes used a nearby telephone to summon the police ambulance-car, and Frank was taken to the County Hospital with multiple injuries to his head, neck and body. He never regained consciousness, and sadly passed away 15 minutes after his arrival.

A Coroner's Inquest was held the following day where Jennie Herrick testified that she had been to the mortuary, and identified the body as being that of her brother Frank. Mr Russon deposed that his bull was four years old. He added that it had always been quiet, and was used to being led about, The next witness was Mr Francis who explained that, whilst chasing the heifer, he lost sight of Frank and was completely unaware of what had happened until sometime after the incident.

After hearing evidence from Mr and Mrs Oakes, the Coroner then heard from Constable Newham of the Lindsey Police. The officer said that when he went to Riseholme Road at 6:10 pm, the bull was still fastened to the tree. He went on to say, "It appeared to be very restless and in a wild state." He also noticed that an iron fence nearby was very badly damaged and added, "The three bottom rails were broken, and the top one bent. It appeared from the way in which the fence was bent, that the man had been driven against the railing and, with no means of escape, he was at the mercy of the bull."

In summing-up, the Coroner turned to Thomas Oakes and said, "I should like to compliment you on the presence of mind and pluck that you showed." A verdict of "Death by misadventure" was then recorded.

Frank was 53 years old and had never married. He was laid to rest in plot P111 at St Swithin's Cemetery, Lincoln.

Primary source: Retford and Worksop Herald, June 7th, 1927

Footnote:

Coultham Street was situated between Canwick Road and Clifton Street. It was demolished in the 1950s as part of the Pelham Bridge development.

54: Joseph Wilfred Shelton

Lincoln - 1927: Accused of Theft

Joseph was born in North Hykeham, on November 26th, 1895 and was the youngest of five children belonging to Samuel (a railway platelayer) and Fanny Shelton. Sadly, Joseph's mother died unexpectedly in 1898, aged 33.

In 1900, Joseph's father married Martha Topliss, a single woman from Harmston, who took on the responsibility for raising her step-children at their new home on Raglan Street, Lincoln (see footnote). By 1903, Martha had given Samuel two more children but tragically, she passed away in 1905, aged 36.

The 1911 census shows that Joseph was still living with his family on Raglan Street, and he was working as a telegram messenger boy. However, when war was declared against Germany, he volunteered to fight for his country. In the first instance, he served with the Royal Irish Fusiliers, but he transferred to the Machine Gun Corps when it was established in October 1915. He served right through the conflict without a scratch, and married his sweetheart, Mabel Pinder, after the Armistice in November, 1918.

The couple established their home at 25, Motherby Hill, and Joseph took various labouring jobs, to put food on the table. However, in April 1923, he gained employment with the General Post Office (GPO) as a postman. The work was not well-paid, but it provided a regular income, and they decided to start a family. Their daughter, Audrey, was born in July 1924.

In the 1920s, the postal service in the U.K. was held in high esteem by the public. With four deliveries a day, it was not uncommon to post a letter in the morning and to receive a reply that same evening. The service was extremely reliable and any reports of letters having gone astray were taken very seriously.

During June, 1927, there was a flurry of reports about missing letters in the Lincoln area, and these were passed through to head office in London for investigation. A pattern soon emerged, and the common denominator seemed to be Joseph Shelton.

On the morning of Friday, July 1st, 1927, two men travelled from London to Lincoln by express train. One of the men was George Muir, a senior clerk from the GPO, and the other was Detective Constable Tom Price, from Scotland Yard. They made their way to Lincoln's main post office on Guildhall Street, where they interviewed Joseph in a room on the third floor. Joseph seemed unfazed by the questions, and completely denied the allegations.

When the interview ended, the detective started completing a document which recorded Joseph's antecedent history, and included information about his date of birth, place of birth, and previous employments. Around 1:30pm, whilst the officer was writing details about Joseph's army service, Joseph rose from his chair and sauntered towards the window. The window was closed but, without saying another word, Joseph dived head-first through the glass, and fell 50 feet onto the ground below. He was killed instantly.

A Coroner's Inquest was held the following day, where Daniel Shelton gave evidence that he had identified the body as being that of his brother, Joseph. George Muir and Tom Price both testified to the effect that Joseph had seemed quite rational during the interview and there was nothing about his demeanour which gave them cause to think he was troubled in any way.

The Coroner then heard from Doctor Lambert who said he had examined Joseph's body and concluded that death would have been instantaneous due to an extensive fracture of the skull. He went on to say that any man who spontaneously dived out of a third-floor window, "Must be completely out of his mind." A verdict of "Suicide whilst of unsound mind" was then recorded.

What happened next?

Joseph was buried in plot Y120 at Canwick Road New Cemetery on July 5th, 1927. He was 32 years old.

The 1939 Register shows that Mabel and their daughter, Audrey, were still living at 39 Motherby Hill. Mabel never remarried and passed away in Nottingham in 1944, aged 49.

Audrey married Peter Gerald Key (a Leading Aircraftsman in the RAF), at St Martin's Church, Lincoln, in February 1944. Records show that the couple had at least four children. In later life they lived at 109, St Giles Avenue, Sleaford, where Audrey passed away in 1977, aged 53.

Primary source: Retford & Worksop Herald, July 5th, 1927.

Footnote:

Raglan Street was a row of terraced houses off Waterloo Street, in the Boultham district of Lincoln. It was demolished during the 1980s and Morrisons supermarket now occupies the site.

55: Arthur Lewin

Lincoln - 1928: A Plucky Gatekeeper

Arthur Lewin was born at Tempsford, Bedfordshire, on May 14th, 1861. He was one of three sons born to William (a market gardener with 15 acres) and Hannah Lewin. After leaving school, he spent the next 10 years of his life living with his parents, and working on their land. He left home in his mid-twenties and became a signalman on the railway at Caythorpe, Lincolnshire. Then, on June 2nd, 1885, he married a farmer's daughter, named Susannah Garton, at St Andrew's Church, Helpringham (near Sleaford).

The 1901 census shows that Arthur was still working as a signalman and that the couple were living at 28, Vernon Street, Lincoln. Tragically, Susannah passed away unexpectedly in 1908. She was 48 years old and was laid to rest in plot C107, at Canwick Road Old Cemetery. The couple did not have any children.

Arthur continued working for the railway company for the next 2 decades and by 1928, in his 67th year, he was one of the gatekeepers at the busy Durham Ox level crossing in Lincoln (see footnote). Shortly after 8:40pm on Thursday, October 18th, 1928, Arthur had closed the gates to allow a train to pass. At that point, he saw an elderly man, named John Elvin Jackson, walk through a pedestrian wicket gate on the Canwick Road side of the crossing. Arthur shouted a warning, but the man sauntered onto the tracks directly into the path of an oncoming engine. Perceiving the danger, Arthur dashed forward in an attempt to pull Mr Jackson out of harm's way. Tragically, the engine hit both men. Mr Jackson was killed outright, and Arthur received serious injuries to his left arm. Arthur was rushed to hospital where his left arm had to be amputated below the elbow.

A Coroner's Inquest was held two days later at the Sessions House. Arthur was too poorly to attend. The court was informed that Mr Jackson was a 66-year-old pattern maker, who was completely deaf. He had spent Thursday evening working on his allotment, and was making his way home to 1, Spa Buildings, on Rosemary Lane, when the incident took place.

The Jury then heard from John Nelsey, of 43, Brancaster Drive, Lincoln. Mr Nelsey testified that he was a signalman at the Pelham Street signal box and, that at 8:44pm, he gave the signal for the gates to be closed to allow an engine and two wagons to pass. Once the gates had been closed, he gave a signal for the engine to proceed over the crossing. He watched as the engine approached the crossing at a speed of around five miles per hour, and then saw Mr Jackson start to cross the lines. Mr Nelsey shouted a warning, but this had no effect. He then saw Mr Lewin dash onto the tracks and both men were struck by the engine. When questioned by the Coroner, Mr Nelsey explained that the small wicket gates did not have any form of locking mechanism.

The Jury returned a verdict of, "Accidental Death," with a recommendation that, "Someone should always be on duty at the wicket gates whenever a train was about to pass."

What happened next?

John Elvin Jackson was married with three grown up children and was buried in plot O 71 in St Swithin's Cemetery, Lincoln. His wife, Alice, continued living at 1, Spa Buildings until her death in 1954, aged 78. She was laid to rest in the same grave as her husband.

On March 27th, 1929 Arthur Lewin travelled to St James's Palace, London where the Prince of Wales, invested him with the Edward Medal (see footnote), in recognition of his bravery in trying to rescue Mr Jackson.

On May 7th, 1929, at a meeting of the Lincoln City Council, the Mayor presented Arthur with a framed certificate from the Carnegie Hero Trust Fund. He also announced that the fund had awarded Arthur the sum of 8 shillings per week, for the remainder of his life, in recognition of his selfless bravery.

Arthur went on to have a very long life, but passed away in June 1950, aged 89 years. He was laid to rest at Canwick Road Old Cemetery, where he shares a grave with his wife Susannah.

Primary source: Sheffield Daily Telegraph, October 19th, 1928

Footnotes:

The Durham Ox level crossing was on Pelham Street, Lincoln. The crossing had double gates which were operated manually and, as it was located near to the convergence of six different railway tracks, it was probably the busiest level crossing in Lincolnshire. When Queen Elizabeth II opened Pelham Bridge in 1958, the crossing became redundant, and it was removed.

The Edward Medal was instigated in 1907, to recognise acts of bravery by miners and quarrymen, but was later expanded to encompass other sectors of industry. The medal was commonly known as "The worker's Victoria Cross".

56: Robert Howden

Heighington - 1931: A Bathing Bridegroom

Robert was born during the spring of 1908, to Frederick (a labourer) and Mary Howden. He was the youngest of three boys and the family lived on Bridge Street, Lincoln. By 1911 however, the three boys and their mother were living apart from their father. He had taken lodgings on Cross Street, Lincoln, and they were living with Mary's parents in Heighington. Robert spent the rest of his childhood in Heighington and, after leaving school, he gained employment as a packer at Clayton Dewandre's Engineering Works. In his spare time, he kept wicket for the village cricket team, where he had the reputation of being, "absolutely fearless."

In 1931, he started courting Esther Dunwell. Esther was originally from Sheffield, but she was in service with Colonel Ward at 3, Minster Yard, Lincoln. The pair were well-matched. She accepted Robert's proposal, and they made arrangements to get married in the parish church at Washingborough during "trip's week" later that year (see footnote).

Robert was not a regular church-goer, but on Sunday, June 28th, 1931, he made a point of attending the morning service to hear the third reading of their wedding banns. Due to work commitments, Esther was unable to attend, but they made arrangements to meet at the village bus stop at 5:30pm that afternoon.

It was a beautiful sunny day so, after lunch, Robert met up with his friend, Horace Leachman, and suggested that they should go for a swim in the river to cool down. The two young men cycled to the nearby River Witham, changed into their bathing costumes and entered the water. Horace started swimming downstream but within 20 seconds he heard shouts of alarm from the bank. He turned around and saw Robert splashing about near the centre of the river. Horace initially thought Robert was larking about, but it was soon clear that he was in distress, and he watched as Robert disappeared under the water. Horace dived, grabbed hold of Robert's arm, pulled him to the surface, and started pulling him towards the bank. However, Robert then clambered onto Horace's back, and the pair both plummeted to the bottom of the river. Horace used all of his strength to push-off from the river bed but, as he did so, he lost his grip on Robert. Horace re-surfaced a few yards from the bank but there was no sign of Robert. Horace, and other swimmers in the vicinity, carried on searching for Robert, but their efforts were in vain. His body was recovered at 5pm that evening by boatmen using a dragline. Meanwhile, whilst Esther was waiting patiently for Robert at the bus stop, she was given the sad news that her fiancée had drowned.

A Coroner's Inquest was held the following day. The Jury heard from several young men who had witnessed the tragedy, before Horace took the oath and tearfully related the sequence of events. Doctor W Parker then told the Jury that he had conducted a post mortem examination of Robert's body. His stomach contained a large quantity of undigested food and, in his opinion, death was due to, "The shock of relatively-cold water in the presence of a full stomach." The Jury returned a verdict of "Death by misadventure," and the Coroner praised Horace for his courageous attempt to save the life of his friend.

Robert Howden was 23 years old, and was laid to rest at St John the Evangelist Church in Washingborough.

What happened to Horace?

Herbert "Horace" Leachman married Sylvia Millson in 1935. The 1939 register lists his occupation as being a "miller's office manager". It also shows they were living on Washingborough Road, Heighington, and had two young children. In later life, Horace lived at 1, Harpswell Road in Lincoln. He passed away, aged 72, on July 17th, 1981.

What happened to Esther?

Esther eventually found the courage to meet other men and she married Sydney Staniforth (a general labourer) at Lincoln in October 1933. The 1939 Register shows they were living at Laurel Cottage, Main Road, Washingborough. The couple did not have any children and she was widowed in 1981. Esther reached the age of 85 before passing away in Lincoln in 1993.

Primary source: Lincolnshire Echo, June 30th, 1931

Footnote:

Trip's week in Lincoln took place for seven days at the end of July and the beginning of August every year. Factories and shops would close, and most workers would flock to the East Coast for a holiday.

57: David Shoebottom

Lincoln - 1932: A Brave Rescue

David was born in Manchester on July 8th, 1892. He was one of seven children born to Joseph (a warehouseman) and Alice Shoebottom who lived at 5, Frampton Street in Salford. After leaving school, David completed his apprenticeship as a turner in one of the local factories.

During The Great War the industrial might of Victorian Lincoln was harnessed to produce military hardware. David responded to a national appeal for skilled workers and moved to the city. He soon gained employment at Messrs Ruston and Co as a turner in their munitions factory. He remained in the city after the war.

During the afternoon of Thursday, February 18th, 1932, David walked from his lodgings at 26, Montague Street, onto Waterside North, where he saw several young boys playing in the street at the end of Duckering's Passage. He then heard a shout that one of the boys had fallen into the river. David rushed to the spot and jumped, fully-clothed, into the icy water. As a non-swimmer, David struggled to keep his own head above water, but he managed to catch hold of the boy's clothing and dragged him to the side. The pair were then helped out of the water by other men who had heard the commotion. The boy, who was about six years old, was completely unharmed, but has never been publicly identified.

On March 24th, 1932, the Mayor of Lincoln presented David with a Testimonial on Parchment from the Royal Humane Society and said, "Owing to the depth of the water, and there being nothing on the river wall to get hold of, David Shoebottom ran a great risk of being drowned himself. He showed great British courage." A reporter, who was present, recorded David's reply. He said, "I only did my duty as a citizen and, if the occasion arises, I would do it again."

What happened next?

The 1939 Register shows David was lodging with the Hatfield family at 21, Croft Street, Lincoln, but details of his later life are unknown.

He never married and died in Lincoln in 1977, aged 84 years.

Primary source; Lincolnshire Echo, March 24th 1932

58: Gladys Mary Field

Lincoln - 1932: Trafficked Babies

Gladys was born at Manchester in 1901, and was one of four children born to Joseph and Agnes Olivant. By 1911 the family had relocated to Scunthorpe where the children had a strict Christian upbringing on account of their father being the pastor at the town's Bethel Mission on Gilliatt Street.

After leaving school, Gladys trained as a short-hand typist and worked at Messrs J Brown & Co (steelworks) for several years. She developed a strong religious vocation herself and, in her spare time, acted as an unpaid missionary and organist at her father's chapel. Gladys remained single until she was in her mid-twenties before marrying Walter Field (a joiner and undertaker) at the Scunthorpe Wesleyan Chapel, in June, 1927. Their daughter Betty was born the following year.

By November 1930, the Field family were living at 9, Moor Street, Lincoln, and became victims of The Great Depression. When Walter became unemployed, they were unable to pay the rent, and struggled to put food on the table. It was at this low point in their lives that Gladys saw an advertisement in the Lincolnshire Echo, from an unmarried mother looking for someone to adopt her new-born baby boy, named John. Walter and Gladys responded to the advertisement (using a fictitious name), adopted the boy and received the sum of £25. The couple then adopted a girl named Frances and received a similar sum towards her upkeep.

At some point over the next few months Gladys and John realised that they could earn a decent living by way of adopting children, and they devised a cunning plan. The couple moved to Wadhurst, Sussex, where they scoured the local papers looking for unwanted babies to adopt. Between March 12th, and April 18th, they adopted three new-born babies and received cash payments for each one. However, instead of caring for these vulnerable infants, they treated them like a commodity. Gladys and Walter "farmed" the babies out to other families on the promise that they would pay a small amount every week towards their upkeep.

The couple then adopted a fourth baby named John Edgeler from an unmarried mother at Pembury, and received £26 for their "act of charity". However, despite repeated requests, Gladys and Walter had not actually paid anything towards the upkeep of the first three babies, and simply pocketed their "profit". Complaints were eventually made to the authorities who commenced an investigation into the circumstances. By the end of 1931, the pair realised they were under suspicion and left the area for good.

On January 11th, 1932, the couple took lodgings at 29, Chaucer Drive, Lincoln, bringing three children with them, the youngest of whom was baby John Edgeler. Tragically, within a few weeks of their arrival, John passed away overnight. The following morning, Gladys and Walter placed the dead baby in a perambulator and, as they were leaving the house, they told their landlady that the boy was asleep and they were taking him to Glady's sister in London. This was a lie, and John was never seen again.

By May 1932, police in Sussex had become involved and circulated details of Gladys and Walter to police forces around the country in the Police Gazette. An officer in Lincoln recognised the couple and they were taken into custody. When interviewed, they made a full admission about their criminal enterprise and Gladys also admitted that she had wrapped baby John Edgeler in brown paper, and dumped his body into the River Trent at Gainsborough. She claimed that John had simply died in his sleep.

Walter and Gladys appeared at Lincoln Magistrates' Court on May 17th, 1932 charged with several offences of obtaining money by false pretences, and one of unlawfully disposing of John's body. The couple both pleaded Guilty. The court heard that police had dragged the River Trent at Gainsborough but had not found John's body. The Court was also informed that, as a result of Gladys and Walter's full co-operation, all of the other children involved had been traced and were now in places of safety. In passing sentence, the Chairman of the Bench said, "You have been found Guilty of several disgraceful and heartless transactions, and I do not know whether we have ever had to deal with a more unsavoury case." Gladys and Walter were both committed to prison for twelve months with hard labour.

What happened next?

The couple stayed together after their release and the 1939 Register shows that were living at Sherwood Vale in Scunthorpe along with their daughter Betty. Walter and Gladys both went on to have long lives and there were no further accusations of criminal conduct. Walter died in Hull in 1984, aged 81. Gladys died in Beverly the following year aged 84.

Their daughter, Betty, married in Scarborough in 1951 but details of her life beyond this point have been kept private.

Full details of the surviving children involved in the adoption scandal have never been made public.

Primary source: Lincolnshire Standard, May 21st, 1932

59: John William Hill

Lincoln - 1932: A Bent Copper

John was born in Lincoln in 1888, to John (a soldier) and Emily Hill. He spent all of his childhood in the city and joined the 2nd Lincolnshire Regiment after leaving school. When he was discharged in 1913, his conduct was described as exemplary.

He then applied to join the City of Lincoln Police and, with his impeccable record, he was readily accepted. He married Eva Boulton (a locksmith's daughter) in 1919, and children soon followed. By 1932 John and Eva had four children and were living at 12, Goldsmith Walk, in the north of the city. By now, John had completed 19 years of service and was regarded as being a "steady" officer.

Harry Harding owned a small garage on West Parade in Lincoln and, in September 1932, he discovered some money was missing from his till on more than one occasion. The thefts always happened overnight, but it remained a complete mystery how the culprit had gained access as there was no sign of a forced entry. Purely by chance however, he discovered that if bodily pressure was applied to his sliding doors in a certain way, then one of the doors could be partially opened. Mr Harding reported the matter to the police.

During the evening of September 12th, Detective Inspector Birkin and Detective Constable Needham, placed several marked coins in Mr Harding's till. Then, after Mr Harding locked up for the night, they secreted themselves in the adjoining workshop and listened carefully. At 1:20am the two detectives heard the sound of someone pushing at the sliding doors. Upon looking through a window a few minutes later, they saw Constable Hill walking away from the garage. The detectives initially assumed that the sound they heard was attributable to the officer "checking" property on his beat (a normal practice in those days) but, when they looked in the till at 5:30am, they discovered that 22 shillings had been taken.

The detectives rushed to the police station and took Constable Hill to an unoccupied office and told him to empty his pockets. The officer placed 17 shillings on the desk and each of the coins was marked in a certain way. Constable Hill said, "I will admit taking it, Sir."

Constable Harrison then came forward and handed Detective Inspector Birkin two half-crowns (5 shillings) and said that Hill had given him the coins earlier and asked him to place a bet on a horse named Vain Batchelor. However, Constable Hill then tried to implicate Harrison by saying, "You saw me take this money, own up to it".

Constable Hill was then charged with burglary at the garage and Constable Harrison was charged with receiving stolen property. The two officers appeared before the Magistrates later the same morning and were remanded to appear at a higher court. Both officers were granted bail, but the case against Constable Harrison was subsequently discontinued through lack of evidence.

John William Hill appeared before Mr Justice Pritchett at the Lincoln Quarter Sessions, on Wednesday, October 12th, 1932 and pleaded Guilty. A court reporter noticed that Hill was crying in the dock as the Judge said, "The consequences of this are terrible. Apart from anything I may do, you have lost your position in the force and the future for you is as gloomy as it possibly can be. You will go to prison for three months."

What happened next?

In addition to losing his job as a police officer, John Hill also lost his entitlement to a pension. He was only six years away from his retirement when he was convicted.

Eva Hill stood by her husband and they resumed their married life after his release. The 1939 Register shows that the family were then living at 12, Earl Street, Lincoln, and that John was a warehouseman at the Co-op Flour Mill.

John Hill died in Lincoln in 1970, aged 82.

Primary source: Daily Mirror, October 13th, 1932

60: Henry Twiggs

Lincoln - 1933: Liked Young Girls

Henry was born at Southwark (London) on February 6th, 1876, to Edward (a compositor, see footnote) and Mary Ann Twiggs. He had two siblings, and the family lived at 57, Queen's Row, near the Elephant and Castle. After leaving school, Henry followed his father's footsteps and trained as a compositor at a local print works. In 1897 however, he enlisted as a marine in the Royal Navy where he rose to the rank of Sergeant. He served on several warships including the cruiser, HMS Minotaur, which took part in the Battle of Jutland in 1916. He retired in 1922, after 25 years of exemplary service. He then moved to Lincoln to be near his sister Charlotte, and he gained employment with a local printing firm.

By 1931, Henry was lodging at 34, Chaucer Drive, Lincoln, and he struck up a friendship with a woman named Sarah Ann Walker who lived at 197, West Parade, in the city's west end. Sarah was living apart from her husband and had five children, including an eight-year-old illegitimate daughter called Jane (not her real name). Henry informed Sarah that he was very fond of children and asked if he might be allowed to take Jane to the cinema. Sarah agreed.

Over the following months Henry took Jane on day trips to the Lincolnshire coast, where he would treat her by buying clothes, shoes, sweets and toys. Then, on November 5th, 1931, Henry asked if he could take Jane to a bonfire party. Sarah consented and agreed that Jane could stay with Henry overnight. This was the first of many occasions where Henry shared his bed with Jane.

Over the following two years, Jane was a regular visitor at 34, Chaucer Drive, and Henry took her on numerous outings including: trips to the Goose Fair in Nottingham; a sight-seeing day in London and a short holiday to Holland. It seemed that nobody thought it unusual for a man in his fifties to be sharing a bed with a child, until that is, he took his taste for young girls to the next level.

By the beginning of 1933, Henry was encouraging Jane to bring her 11-year-old friend Alice (not her real name) on the outings. Henry carefully groomed Alice by taking the two girls on trips to the cinema and local cafes, and her parents readily agreed to allow Alice to go with Henry and Jane for a weekend in Skegness. Henry booked a room in a guest house on Sandbeck Avenue, and the two girls shared his bed for the entire weekend. The landlady, Hannah Potter, had suspicions about Henry's motives and listened attentively at the door during the evenings whilst Henry played "hospitals" with the two girls. The game involved Henry taking the role of a doctor, and required the two girls to get undressed and allow themselves to be intimately examined. Mrs Potter did not confront Henry at the time, but alerted the police after his departure.

After leaving Skegness, Henry took the two girls back to his room at 34, Chaucer Drive, and spent another night with them. Their boisterous activities attracted the attention of another lodger named James Hall. He was awoken by the sound of one of the girls crying out, followed by the sound of squealing laughter and kissing. Mr Hall reported his concerns to the police the following morning.

The case was passed to Detective Inspector Birkin who visited 34, Chaucer Drive, on the night of September 11th, 1933. He asked the landlord to be shown to Henry's room and, when he entered, he found Henry and Jane in bed together. He instructed Jane to get dressed and took her to her mother's home. The officer returned to 34, Chaucer Drive, on September 13th, and arrested Henry. When charged, Henry replied, "I absolutely deny it, but I know the evidence is against me". The officer then paid a visit to Jane's mother and summonsed her for aiding and abetting Henry.

Henry and Sarah appeared at the Lincoln Assizes on Saturday, November 4th, 1933. The case for the prosecution was outlined by Mr Carter KC who said, "The conduct of a man of 57, towards two little girls of 10 and 11, was of a grossly indecent character, and he has debauched these two little girls." He added that, in respect of Sarah Walker, "It was a case of whether she knew what was going on." After hearing evidence from the principal witnesses, members of the public (including reporters) were cleared from court to allow Jane and Alice to give evidence. Their sensitive testimony has never been published.

Henry was represented by Mr Jenkins KC, who outlined the fact that Henry's character was impeccable beyond reproach, and that his relationship with the two girls was of a completely innocent and platonic nature. When Henry took the stand he said, "I never intentionally assaulted them in any way, and there is a misconstruction on the part of the girl's evidence altogether." He went onto describe, what he called, a pure-minded love for the girls.

Sarah Walker was represented by Mr Robinson KC who outlined the impoverished circumstances of his client. Sarah gave evidence in her defence and said she had known Henry for two years and had been told that he was very respectable. Sarah went on to say that she was very poor, and was grateful to anyone who showed kindness to Jane. However, when Sarah was cross-examined by Mr Carter, Sarah admitted that she knew Henry only had one bed but, "Never thought to ask how they slept."

The Jury found Henry and Sarah Guilty of all charges. In passing sentence Mr Justice Hume-Williams said, "I think this is a horrible case. Such men are pests of society." Henry was sentenced to two years imprisonment with hard labour. Sarah was jailed for six months, but she subsequently lodged an appeal and her conviction was overturned.

What happened next?

The real names of "Jane" and "Alice" have never been released into the public domain. The author has chosen not to speculate which of Sarah Walker's daughters was involved. After her release from custody, Sarah Walker spoke of moving to Nottingham under an assumed name. Details of her life beyond this point are unknown.

When Henry Twiggs was released in 1935, he rented a room at 1, Burns Gardens in Lincoln. However, two years of hard labour in prison had taken a heavy toll on his health, and he passed away, aged 61, on December 3rd, 1937. He was laid to rest in plot F9 at Newport Cemetery in Lincoln.

Primary sources:
Skegness News, October 4th, 1933
Skegness News, November 8th, 1933

Footnote:

A compositor is a person who arranges the words or pictures of a book, magazine, or newspaper before printing can take place.

61: Charles Oldham

Lincoln - 1935: A Tragic Coincidence

Charles was born in Harmston, some five miles south of Lincoln, in 1887. He was the youngest of 5 children born to George (a platelayer on the railway) and Rebecca Oldham who lived on School Lane, Harmston.

Tragedy first hit the family in 1899, when Charles was 12. His older brother, George, had followed his father's footsteps and worked as a platelayer on the railways. At 9am, on January 29th, George was one of ten men engaged in repairing the down-line at Peacock Bridge near Peterborough. It was a cold, misty morning and when a heavy goods train passed on the up-line, it emitted dense volumes of smoke which further reduced visibility. Seconds later, a light engine came along the down-line. Eight of the men jumped clear but, once the smoke had cleared, they found that George and one of his colleagues had been killed by the engine. George was 24 years old, and had never married.

After leaving school, Charles chose a less dangerous occupation, and served his apprenticeship as a blacksmith. He married Edith Taylor in 1914, and the couple raised 3 children at 9, Urban Street, in Bracebridge.

On the morning of Tuesday, March 19th, 1935, Charles and his 14-year-old son, Jack were both working for a nurseryman, named Wilfred Rowland, from Saxilby. Their last job before lunch was to collect plants and fertiliser from the company's premises in Harby, and deliver them to some allotments, beyond the railway line, at the end of Urban Street. Wilfred stopped his lorry at the unmanned railway crossing and asked Jack to open the crossing gates. Jack jumped from the cab and, as he opened the nearest gate, he saw a train approaching. He shouted to Wilfred, "A train is coming about a quarter of a mile away." Wilfred replied, "We shall beat the train."

Jack opened the furthest gate and watched as Wilfred drove the lorry onto the crossing. By this time the train was perilously close, and as the lorry crossed over the line, the engine smashed into the lorry's cab. The lorry burst into flames and was pushed some 400 yards down the track before the train could be brought to a complete stop. Charles and Wilfred were both killed instantly.

A Coroner's Inquest was held two days later, where Jack emotionally testified about what had happened. The court then heard from Arthur Hall, who said he was driving the train on the day in question. He had been driving along this section of track for over 15 years and sounded the train's whistle twice as he approached the crossing at a speed of 45 miles an hour. He described how the lorry pulled onto the track directly in front of him, leaving him with absolutely no time to react. The Jury then heard from Detective Constable Needham, who said that the two deceased men had been mutilated beyond recognition, and could only be identified from various belongings which were in their possession. The Jury returned a verdict of, "Death by misadventure," and attached no blame to the driver of the train.

What happened next?

Charles Oldham was 47 years old, and was laid to rest shortly after the Inquest.

Wilfred Rowland was a 29-year-old married man who lived on William Street, Saxilby, with his wife Ivy. He was buried at St Botolph's Church, Saxilby, on March 22nd, 1935.

Records relating to Jack Oldham are inconclusive.

Primary source: Nottingham Journal, March 20th, 1935

62: John Dixon

Lincoln - 1939: The George Cross

John was born on June 23rd, 1913, in Bradford. He was one of three children born to Frederick (an out-patient clerk) and Matilda Dixon. By 1915, the family had relocated to Grantham. When he was 14, John then moved to Lincoln where he served an apprenticeship as an electrician with Messrs Robey & Co. In 1933, he married Edith Ethel Scott, at Lincoln. The couple made their home at 63, Great Northern Terrace, Lincoln, and their daughter was born later the same year.

During the afternoon of Thursday, February 16th, 1939, John was working at Robey's Foundry in a factory known as the Globe Works. At about 3pm, he was remotely monitoring the electrical equipment associated with an overhead crane. The crane was operated by a man, named Whittaker, who was perched in his cab some 40 feet above the shop floor. The crane lifted a heavy crucible, full of molten metal, and Mr Whittaker then manipulated the controls to carefully pour the molten metal into a large mould. For reasons which have not been documented, an accident occurred, and molten metal spurted 40 feet into the air. Within seconds, the factory roof, and the gantry supporting the overhead crane, were ablaze.

John, who was in a position of comparative safety, watched as Mr Whittaker climbed out of his cab. However, his clothes had caught alight and he collapsed onto a high-level walkway. At this point, John ran through leaping flames to Mr Whittaker's aid, and smothered his blazing clothing with his own jacket. John then physically carried Mr Whittaker along a gantry, which gave access to the roof. He then worked his way along a gulley between two sections of the roof, before carrying Mr Whittaker down a long ladder to safety.

Upon reaching the ground, John insisted that first aiders should treat Mr Whittaker first. Mr Whittaker went on to make a full recovery. However, John was badly burned on his arms and the upper part of his body. He required hospital treatment, and was unable to return to work for ten weeks.

What happened next?

In October 1939, the Mayor of Lincoln presented John with a medal, and the sum of £5 from the Society for the Protection of Life from Fire. Then, on February 23rd, 1940, the London Gazette announced that John had been awarded the Edward Medal in recognition of his courage.

When the award was discontinued in 1971, surviving recipients were invited to exchange their award for its modern replacement. On November 9th, 1972, John Dixon travelled to Buckingham Palace where Queen Elizabeth II, invested him with the George Cross.

In later life, John lived at 107, Cannon Street, Lincoln, where he passed away on April 13th, 1984. He was 70 years old and was buried in plot 01103 at Newport Cemetery. His wife, who was always known as Ethel, died in 1998, aged 84 and was interred in the same grave.

Primary source: Nottingham Journal, February 24th, 1940

63: Sheila Caygill

Lincoln - 1940: An Evacuee

Sheila was born at Barton upon Irwell (Greater Manchester) on May 15th, 1928, and was one of three children whose parents were Frederick (a merchant seaman) and Dorothy Caygill. It is not known how Sheila spent the first 11 years of her life. However, the 1939 Register shows that the family were living at the Parklands Hotel, Boultham Park Road, Lincoln. The building was brand new, and Frederick Caygill had been appointed as its first landlord.

Sheila, and her older sister Betty, both attended South Park School, but their studies were interrupted during the summer of 1940, when they learned that they were to be evacuated from Lincoln due to the risk of bombing by the Luftwaffe. Most of the 3.5 million children who were evacuated from cities during the conflict, were sent to host families who lived in quiet rural areas around the UK, but the Caygill family decided the safest option for Sheila and Betty was for them to go to Canada as part of a scheme devised by the Children's Overseas Reception Board.

The two sisters travelled to Liverpool by train and were put aboard a Dutch-owned transatlantic liner, SS Volendam (15,434 tons). The ship set sail on August 29th, 1940, with 879 souls on board including: 273 crew members, 286 adult passengers, and 320 children. The captain, Jan Wepster, steered a northerly course, and joined 32 other vessels to form convoy OB205. The convoy, escorted by the destroyer HMS Sabre, then headed in a westerly direction towards the Canadian coast.

Meanwhile, during the early hours of August 31st, 1940, at least four German U-Boats were lurking some 200 miles west of Bloody Foreland (County Donegal) waiting for the opportunity to strike. Albert Schnee, the commander of U-60, shadowed the convoy and singled-out the Volendam. He fired two torpedoes and one of them exploded, just below the waterline, near number one hold. The impact made a hole some 50 feet wide and the ship started to list precariously. The captain gave the order to abandon ship.

Sheila and Betty were fast asleep, but were awakened by the sound of the explosion, "which seemed to shake the whole ship." Alarm bells started ringing, and the sisters were told to go to the ship's library, which was their designated assembly station. The sisters were both provided with life jackets, taken to the lifeboats, and lowered into the ocean.

As the lifeboat bobbed around on the choppy sea, a single voice uttered the words, "Our father, who art in heaven." The other occupants of the boat then joined-in and they collectively prayed for their salvation. To lighten the mood, one of the crew then started singing "Roll out the barrel" and other popular songs, until they were picked-up by the oil-tanker, Valdemosa, some 60 minutes later. The tanker picked up more survivors from other lifeboats and Sheila later recalled, "There were 130 of us on board the rescue ship. The sailors were very kind to us. They gave up their beds, and shared their food with us. We landed in Scotland two days later."

Sheila and Betty were placed on a train to Doncaster along with a chaperone, and three other girls from Lincoln (see footnote). They arrived home shortly after 6pm on Wednesday, September 4th. They excitedly related their tale to a newspaper reporter the following day, and said they were quite willing to have another attempt at travelling to Canada. However, their father said he had been torpedoed twice during The Great War and he explicitly forbade them from sailing on another ship.

What happened next?

Captain Wepster stayed on the Volendam with a skeleton crew. They somehow managed to keep her afloat. She was then towed by a tug, and beached on the Isle of Bute. Of the 879 people on board the ship, there had been only one casualty (a steward drowned after missing his footing whilst descending a rope ladder). Convoy OB 205 continued towards Canada but, despite extensive depth-charging operations by the Royal Navy, four other ships from the convoy were sunk within a few hundred miles of the Irish coast, and a fifth was damaged near the Canadian coast.

What happened to Sheila?

Sheila went on to have a very full life. She married Bernard Banks (an engineer) at Newark in 1948, and the couple had two children. Sheila, and the children, followed Bernard as his work took him around the world. The family lived in Iran in the early 1950s but they had to be evacuated (by aeroplane) due to civil unrest. They then lived in Ghana for 16 years before moving to Nigeria. They returned to Lincoln in the 1960s but, after Bernard's retirement, they relocated to Aylesbury in Buckinghamshire. Sheila was widowed when Bernard passed away in 1995. Records of Sheila's life after this point are somewhat obscure, but if she is still alive, she would now be in her 95th year.

What happened to her sister Betty?

Betty Caygill married Peter Pickering at Scunthorpe in 1946, and their first child was born in York in 1948. They had a daughter whilst living at Ealing (London), in 1949, but the author has been unable to establish any facts about Betty's life beyond this point.

The author has chosen to respect the privacy of Sheila and Betty's children.

Primary sources:
Lincolnshire Echo, September 5th, 1940
Lincolnshire Echo, September 20th, 1989
En.wikipedia.org (SS Volendam)
www.uboat.net

Footnotes:

On September 17th, 1940, the steam ship, City of Benares, was conveying 123 children to Canada when it was attacked by a U-Boat in the middle of the night. The order was given to abandon ship and lifeboats were launched. However, the ship sank quickly, and 258 people (including 77 of the children), lost their lives. Unsurprisingly, these two incidents caused the Children's Overseas Reception Board to reconsider their policy, and no more children were officially evacuated across the Atlantic beyond this point.

The other girls from Lincoln who were on SS Volendam were sisters, Joan Mary Walker (aged 12) and Margaret Walker (aged 15) from West Parade, Lincoln, along with Myra Joyce Edwards (aged 12) of Lindum Road. Records relating to the future lives of these 3 girls are inconclusive.

The Volendam was refloated in 1941, and towed to Camel Laird Shipyard at Birkenhead. When it entered dry dock, workers discovered that an unexploded torpedo was lodged in its bow. The torpedo's malfunction undoubtedly saved the ship, and hundreds of lives. After undergoing repairs, the Volendam was used as a troop ship for the remainder of the war, and it is estimated that over 100,000 soldiers were transported on her. She was put back into use as a liner in 1948 and was finally sent to the breaker's yard in 1952.

The Parklands Hotel closed in 2008. It was subsequently demolished and a Co-op convenience store has been built on the site.

64: Lena May Thacker

Lincoln - 1943: A Blazing House

Lena was born at South Willingham, near Louth, on May 2nd, 1905. She was one of eight children and their parents were Newell (an agricultural labourer) and Elizabeth Anderson. Lena's father worked for Baron and Lady Heneage of Hainton Hall, and the family lived in one of the farm cottages on South Road in the village. Lena remained single until she was in her mid-twenties before marrying James Robert Thacker (a railway shunter) at St Faith's Church, Lincoln, on October 25th, 1930.

The couple had two daughters during the 1930s and, by the outbreak of World War 2, the family were living at 24, Highfield Avenue, in the Boultham area of Lincoln. In March 1939, Lena's friend, Gwendoline Whitby, gave birth to an illegitimate baby boy named Lawrence. She was unable to look after the child herself, and it was agreed that Lena and Robert would adopt him. In 1940, Lena then gave birth to another child of her own, named Anthony.

Gwendoline Whitby made a habit of visiting 24, Highfield Avenue every Friday evening to visit Lena, and to see Lawrence. Friday, June 11th, 1943, was no different. On this occasion, Lena's two eldest girls were staying at a relative's house and her husband was at work (see footnote). Shortly after 4pm, Lena was in the kitchen preparing tea for Gwendoline and the two children, when she heard the loud roar of an aeroplane's engines. She rushed outside to investigate when, at that very moment, a Lancaster Bomber crashed directly onto her home and instantly burst into flames.

William Chester of 20, Highfield Avenue, was on his way home from work when he witnessed the crash, and saw Lena rush into the burning house. He then watched with horror as part of the building collapsed on her a few moments later. After ensuring his own wife and children were safe, Mr Chester went to the rear of Lena's house and heard the sound of terrified children screaming from inside. Together with a man named Ernest Wing from Westwick Gardens, Mr Chester tried to batter his way through the back door, but their path was blocked by debris. Mr Chester then went around to a part of the house which was still standing and found the bathroom window was open.

Lawrence and Anthony were both stood in the empty bath tub, but their clothing was alight and they were shrieking aloud. Lena Thacker was on her knees against the bathroom door. The lower half of her body was trapped by burning debris and she shouted, "Save the children". The two men reached through the open window, rescued the two boys, and beat out the flames with their bare hands. The men then went back to the window to help Lena, but there had been a further collapse and she was no longer visible.

Although 24, Highfield Avenue took the brunt of the impact, the houses at 22, 25, and 27 were also totally destroyed. Emergency services attended promptly and, after extinguishing the fires, they set about the grim task of recovering bodies. Lena and Gwendoline's charred remains were recovered from number 22, and the bodies of six aircrew were also found amongst the wreckage of the Lancaster. Tragically, they also found the body of 12-year-old Margaret Marriott under the rubble at 25, Highfield Avenue. Her parents had left the house 30 minutes before the Lancaster crashed, leaving Margaret to do her homework in the kitchen.

Numerous people were taken to hospital with burn injuries including the Bishop family from 22, Highfield Avenue, along with the two boys rescued from number 24. Sadly, Lawrence Whitby passed away within a few hours of his arrival at the hospital and Anthony Thacker succumbed to his injuries three weeks later.

What happened next?

Lena Thacker (aged 38), Anthony Thacker (aged three), and Lawrence Whitby (aged four), share a grave in St Helen's Churchyard in Boultham. Margaret Marriott, who was a pupil at South Park School, was laid to rest in a separate grave in the same churchyard. It is thought that Gwendoline Whitby (aged 42) was cremated.

An investigation by the RAF established that Lancaster Bomber ED833 was on a training flight from nearby RAF Wigsley. The crew's objective was to practice flying on three engines but a technical malfunction caused the aircraft to lose power and crash. A Coroner's Inquest found that the crash was not a consequence of deliberate low-flying and returned a verdict of "Death by misadventure," in respect of each of the 11 victims of the tragedy.

In January 1944, William Chester and Edwin Wing, both received the King's Commendation for Brave Conduct, for their gallant actions in rescuing the two boys from the burning building.

Lena's husband, James, remarried in 1949 and went on to have a long life. He passed away in Lincoln in 1983 aged 78.

Primary source; Lincolnshire Echo, June 12th, 1943

Footnotes:

During World War 2, railway employees and other essential workers were considered to have "reserved occupations" and were not required to join the armed forces.

By a bizarre stroke of luck, one of the aircrew actually survived the crash. Gunner Sergeant C. H. Malkin occupied what was usually the most dangerous position on the aircraft. As the rear turret gunner his life-expectancy was just two weeks but, as the aircraft hit the ground, the rear turret broke loose, and it was found upside-down on a footpath at the rear of 18, Roydon Grove. The airman was badly injured, but he was taken to the County Hospital and eventually made a full recovery.

65: Dorothy Fannen

Lincoln - 1944: Starved her Baby

Dorothy Marea Fannen (sometimes given as Fannan or Fannon) was born on July 13th, 1920, in the Barnsley District and was one of three children born to Christopher and Priscilla Fannen. She spent her early childhood living at Brook Street in Hoyland, near Barnsley but the spectre of death was a constant companion during her young life. Her father (aged 39) passed away when she was just nine years old, and her mother died, after a short illness, when Dorothy was 12. The three children were then informally adopted by Mr & Mrs Walton who lived at 159, West Street, Hoyland. Tragedy struck once again in 1939, when Dorothy's sister, Agnes, passed away at the age of 15.

By 1941, Dorothy had reached the age of majority and she moved to Leeds. Whilst there, she met a 60-year-old man named Arthur Brown. They became intimate, and Dorothy soon discovered she was pregnant. Arthur accepted his responsibilities as the father, but suggested they should move to Lincoln, where they could live beyond the prying eyes of anyone who knew them. The couple rented some rooms at 1, Foster Street, Lincoln, and Dorothy gave birth to a healthy baby boy on March 23rd, 1942. The child weighed 8lb 4oz (3.7kg) and was given the name Adrian Brown.

The relationship between the pair was tempestuous and the police were called to the house on a number of occasions over the next few months. One report suggests that Arthur "thrashed" Dorothy. In the first instance, no formal action was taken by the police other than "giving suitable advice" to both parties. However, on April 5th, 1943, Arthur called the police and accused Dorothy of "going out with friends and leaving the baby unattended in the house." Arthur expanded his concerns by saying, "If he had fallen out of his pram, he might have killed himself." Dorothy then replied, "I wish the bloody thing had, I could then do as I liked." The police officer thought this remark was particularly cold-hearted, and made a note of it in his pocket book. The officer referred the family to the NSPCC and they visited the house on April 13th. They found Adrian to be in good health and established that he weighed 19lb (8.6kg).

A few weeks later, Dorothy discovered she was pregnant again. This came as a shock to Arthur, as he was convinced he could not have been the father. This was the final straw, and he moved to some lodgings in the Brayford area of the city. Despite feeling betrayed, Arthur was determined that his own son should not want for anything, and gave Dorothy £96 (worth around £5,000 today) for his needs. However, as the year progressed, Dorothy refused to accept any further help and she would not allow Arthur to visit Adrian.

This situation continued until November 1943, when Dorothy came to Arthur's lodgings and demanded that he should take the child himself. When Arthur declined, Dorothy declared that, if Arthur would not take the child away from her, she would, "Do away with him, drown him or kill him." Then, during the first week of 1944, Arthur heard rumours to the effect that Adrian had not been seen for several days and he feared that Adrian may have been murdered. He reported his concerns to the police.

Detective Inspector Bradshaw called at the house on January 8th, 1944, and informed Dorothy he had concerns that she had murdered her baby and disposed of the body. Dorothy replied, "I haven't murdered it. It died last Monday, and I have hidden it in a pram in the cellar." The officer went to the cellar and found Adrian's body in his perambulator which had been covered in a rubber sheet. Dorothy then made a statement in which she said, "The child was asleep in his pram at 11:30pm on Sunday, January 2nd. I got up at 9:30am the following morning and cleaned the house for an hour. I then went to the bed-sitting-room and looked at the baby at 10:30am. He was laying on his face as if unconscious." She went on to say that she tried to give Adrian a cup of milk, but he refused it. Adrian never recovered consciousness, and passed away shortly before noon.

Adrian's body was examined by Doctor James Lyons who found his weight was only 10lb 6oz (4.7kg). His stomach, digestive tract and bowel were devoid of any trace of food whatsoever, and the child had the appearance of a skeleton. He concluded that Adrian had been systematically starved over a period of many weeks. Death was, "Due to exhaustion, due to lack of nourishment". Dorothy was arrested and charged with murder. Dorothy, who was now heavily-pregnant, appeared before Magistrates at Lincoln. She was remanded in custody to Birmingham Prison, where she gave birth to her baby on January 18th, 1944. The child was a healthy boy and was given the name Brian Anthony Fannen.

Dorothy was brought before Mr Justice Lewis at the Birmingham Assizes on Thursday, March 16th, 1944. She was defended by Mr Myers Ward KC who argued that this was not a hanging offence, and the charge should be reduced to one of manslaughter. This was accepted by the court, and Dorothy pleaded Guilty. In mitigation, Mr Ward argued that Arthur Brown's violence was the cause of his client's downfall, and she simply struggled to cope on her own. However, in passing sentence, Judge Lewis said Dorothy Fannen, "Was Guilty of a most culpable negligence towards her child, and she had behaved in a most callous manner." He sentenced Dorothy to three years penal servitude and added that Dorothy could care for her new-born child in prison until it was old enough to be taken off her. Dorothy collapsed and had to be carried from the dock.

What happened to her children?

Dorothy's first baby, Adrian Brown was buried on January 12th, 1944, in plot A2014, at Canwick Road Old Cemetery in Lincoln. He was just 21 months old.

Dorothy's second baby, Brian Fannen, was adopted by Lewis (Dorothy's uncle) and Jessie Fannen who lived in Hoyland. Brian married Brenda Taylor at Staincross (Yorkshire) in 1966, and the couple had two children. Brian passed away on September 22nd, 2015, aged 70.

What happened to Dorothy?

Dorothy was released from prison in 1947 and married a man named John Griffiths a few months later, The couple had a son in 1948 but, as it is thought he is still alive, the author has chosen not to publish any further details. John Griffiths died in 1952.

In 1963, Dorothy married Lawrence Dawber at Staincross. Their marriage was childless.

Dorothy passed away in the Barnsley District in 1984. She was 64 years old.

Primary sources:
Lincolnshire Echo: February 15th, 1944
Lincolnshire Echo: March 16th, 1944

Footnote:

The author has liaised with members of the Fannen family in compiling this story, and they are keen to emphasise that Dorothy was not an evil person. She was a single mother, in a strange city, without any support from her family. She had a poor relationship with Adrian's father, which adversely affected her mental health, and this all resulted in her struggling to cope.

66: Jack Kelway

1945 - Welton: A German Attack

Jack was born in Nottingham on February 19th, 1907, to John (a commercial traveller) and Emma Kelway. The 1911 census shows that he was the younger of two children, and the family lived in Arnold. The family subsequently moved to Lincoln, where Jack married Irene Scott in 1931.

By 1939, the couple had two young children (with a third on the way) and were living at 159, Bunkers Hill, Lincoln. Jack worked as a supervisor at Bardney Sugar Beet Factory and was a Special Constable in his spare time. When war was declared against Germany in 1939, Jack joined the Royal Observer Corps. and was assigned to L1 Post at Hackthorn, a few miles to the north of Lincoln. His role was to visually detect aircraft, identify them, and report their number, height and direction of flight to an operations centre.

During the early hours of March 4th, 1945, the skies above Lincolnshire were busy with 150-200 prowling German JU88 night-fighter aircraft. They had been deployed to intercept some 500 allied bombers returning from night-time raids over Germany. Between 0:29am and 1:36am the fighters shot down nine Lancaster and three Halifax Bombers as they came in to land at various airfields across the county. One of the German aircraft was piloted by Feldwebel Heinrich Conze. At 1am Conze intercepted Lancaster NG502 from 460 Squadron and shot it down. It crashed near Barfields House at Langworth, killing two of the crew. Conze then headed towards RAF Scampton looking for other targets.

Meanwhile, at 1am the same morning, Jack Kelway was driving his car along the Welton to Hackthorn Road, to report for duty at his post. His car headlights were "hooded" as required by wartime regulations but Conze spotted the car and decided it was a legitimate target. The JU88 streaked towards the car at ground level and opened fire. Unluckily for the German crew, the night-fighter struck some telegraph wires. The aircraft then cartwheeled into Jack's car, and the force of the impact sent it reeling across two fields. Jack, and the four crew members of the JU88 were all killed instantly.

Jack was buried at Newport Cemetery in Lincoln on March 7th, 1945 with his family and a large number of his Royal Observer Corps colleagues in attendance. He was the only member of the Royal Observer Corps to be killed during the war whilst on duty. The German crew of the JU88 were buried in the graveyard at Scampton Church.

What happened next?

The German graves at Scampton Church are marked with white headstones and have been well-maintained by the War Graves Commission. Sadly, a headstone was not erected over Jack's grave. His widow and children emigrated to Australia shortly after the war, and the grave fell into disrepair.

In October 2017, following a fundraising campaign by a man named Bill Warwick, an impressive headstone was unveiled above Jack's grave. A short ceremony commemorating Jack's life then took place at his graveside. It was attended by representatives from the Royal Observer Corps, Lincolnshire Special Constabulary, and the Commanding Officer of 204 Squadron Air Training Corps. A member of the Lincolnshire Fire and Rescue Band then played the Last Post, Reveille and the National Anthem.

Primary sources:
Daily Mail (online), October 25th, 2017
Royal Observer Corps Association www.roc-heritage.co.uk

67: Marjorie Griffen

Lincoln - 1945: Found in a Shed

Marjorie was born in Lincoln on October 24th, 1922, and was one of six children. Their parents were Charles (a stoker) and Ada Griffen who lived at 153, Goldsmith Walk, Lincoln. After leaving school, Marjorie was employed in the canteen at Clayton Dewandre's factory. She was a bright, happy girl who enjoyed dancing, and sang in the work's band. She liked her job, and enjoyed interacting with the men from the factory floor, one of whom was Walter Harris (an engineer's packer), from Fairfield Street. Walter was some 15 years older than Marjorie, but when he asked her to go to the cinema with him, she readily accepted. By 1945, the pair had been going out for 2 years, and the relationship had become intimate.

At 8:30pm on Monday, August 27th, 1945, Marjorie left 153, Goldsmith Walk for the last time. She told her father that she was going to sleep with a friend whose husband was in the forces. However, at 10:30pm an anonymous telephone call was received at the ambulance station in Lincoln. The caller directed them to, "A very poorly woman, in an old shed, between two houses on Curle Avenue." Ambulance staff eventually found a dilapidated shed, amongst a tangled mass of undergrowth, some 50 feet from the road. When they entered, they found Marjorie's body on an improvised bed, made of planking, over which had been placed a piece of old carpet, with a log forming a pillow. Marjorie's body was removed to the mortuary on Burton Road and a police cordon was established around the scene.

Professor Webster, from the Home Office Forensic Science Laboratories, conducted a post mortem examination. He found that Marjorie was pregnant, and that an unskilled operation had been performed upon her in an attempt to abort the foetus. Marjorie had haemorrhaged and died from the loss of blood. Another scientist, named Dr Holden, took samples of building material from Marjorie's clothing. Police enquiries quickly led them to Walter Harris' door, and he was taken into custody a few hours later. As luck would have it, his trousers had small pieces of building material attached to the fibres. Scientific analysis confirmed a match with the samples taken from Marjorie's clothing.

When interviewed, Harris admitted he had been having an intimate affair with Marjorie and conceded that he had seen her on the night in question. He said that, the last time he saw Marjorie alive, "She was on Curle Avenue in the company of a woman wearing a turban." He went on to say that he subsequently found her lying unconscious, or dead, in the shed and telephoned for an ambulance.

Harris was charged with manslaughter and appeared before Mr Justice Denning at the Lincoln Assizes on Saturday, November 3rd, 1945. The prosecution alleged that Harris had used a syringe in an attempt to abort the pregnancy, and that when Marjorie started bleeding, he fled the scene and called an ambulance. The Jury heard from 15 witnesses, including the two forensic scientists, who gave compelling evidence about 20 exhibits which linked the building materials found on Harris' clothing, with those on Marjorie.

Harris was represented by Mr Myers-Ward KC who tried to portray Marjorie as a woman with loose morals. He claimed there was no evidence that Harris was the father of the unborn child and contended that the forensic evidence linking him to the scene was circumstantial. The Jury retired, and returned a unanimous verdict of, "Guilty," 10 minutes later.

Before the Judge passed sentence, the court heard from Detective Inspector W Bradshaw. The officer informed the court that Harris had married his wife, Doris, in 1939, and they had a three-year-old daughter. He went on to say that Harris had also fathered two illegitimate children, with different women, in 1931 and 1933. In both cases, Harris had simply walked away. Both women had obtained Affiliation Orders which required Harris to support the children, but he had fallen behind with his payments and currently owed over £125 in arrears (equivalent to over £7,500 in today's money). Mr Justice Denman sentenced Harris to six years penal servitude.

What happened next?

Marjorie Griffen was buried in plot J458 at Newport Cemetery, on August 31st, 1945. She was 23 years old.

Harris was divorced by his wife and he returned to Lincoln after his release. Very little has been documented about the remainder of his life, apart from the fact he was admitted to a nursing home in Lincoln shortly before passing away in February 1995, aged 88. He is buried in Newport Cemetery.

Primary sources:
Lincolnshire Echo, August 28th, 1945
Lincolnshire Echo, November 5th, 1945

68: Eileen Breeds

Nettleham - 1946: A Massive Bomb

Eileen was born in Lincoln on January 27th, 1921. Her parents were Cyril (a goods loader on the railway) and Ada Steadman, who lived at 1, Allison Place, in the west end of the city. Eileen was their only child.

Shortly after war was declared in 1939, Eileen left home to join the Women's Auxiliary Air Force (WAAF). By 1943, she was stationed at RAF Locking (near Weston Super Mare), where she met Leading Aircraftsman Ronald Thomas Breeds. The pair were suited, and they got married at St Faith's Church, Lincoln, on October 2nd, 1943. The couple were allocated a house at RAF Locking, and Eileen gave birth to Christopher in December 1944.

In March 1946, Ronald was granted a period of leave, so the family travelled by car to Lincoln to visit Eileen's parents for a few days. Whilst in the city. during the morning of Tuesday, March 19th, Eileen bumped into an old friend who invited them for tea at Nettleham later that afternoon.

On the same morning, Flight Sergeant Alexander Creamer reported for duty at RAF Hemswell, and was ordered to take a low-loader to RAF Faldingworth. Upon arrival, his lorry was loaded with two 4000lb "Blockbuster" bombs, and he was given instructions to covey them to a storage depot at RAF Waddington. This type of bomb was known colloquially by RAF munition specialists as a "cookie" and was regarded as a particularly dangerous load to carry, as it would sometimes explode, even if it was dropped in a supposedly-safe, unarmed, state. With this in mind, Flight Sergeant Creamer carefully checked that his load was secure and set off towards Lincoln shortly after lunch.

Around 1:30pm, Ronald Breeds was driving his car towards Nettleham with Eileen sitting in the front passenger seat. She was cradling 14-month-old Christopher in her arms. Shortly after leaving the outskirts of the city, Ronald was negotiating a series of bends near the Brown Cow Public House, when he saw a low-loader coming towards him at a speed of around 40 m.p.h. The trailer had swung over the central white line, and as the driver wrestled with the steering wheel to regain his correct side of the road, one of the bombs fell off the trailer. Ron braked hard but the impetus of the 4000lb bomb propelled it directly towards their car. It then hit the front of their vehicle with a deafening thud, before rolling harmlessly into the ditch.

All three occupants of the car were thrown forward by the impact. Ronald's head hit the steering wheel causing bruising. Eileen's face, hit the windscreen causing deep cuts, and baby Christopher was knocked unconscious. They were all taken to the County Hospital by ambulance for treatment. Ronald was discharged later the same day, but Eileen and Christopher were admitted for observations. Happily, all three members of the family made a full recovery.

What happened Next?

Flight Sergeant Creamer appeared at Lindsey Magistrates Court on April 26th, 1946, charged with driving at a dangerous speed, and for having an insecure load. He was found Guilty of both charges and fined £4.

By 1967, Ronald Breeds had been promoted to Warrant Officer and the family lived in married quarters at RAF Coningsby. After Ronald's retirement, the couple moved to the Portsmouth area where Eileen passed away in 1981 aged 60. Ronald died in Portsmouth in 1989, aged 69.

Their son, Christopher, subsequently married and had two children but, as it is believed he is still alive, the author has chosen not to disclose any further details.

Primary source: Lincolnshire Echo, March 20th, 1946

Footnote:

Since this incident took place, the main road to Nettleham has been straightened-out. A section of the old road still exists in a cul-de-sac, and is signposted as "Danby Hill".

69: Henry Tyler

Lincoln - 1955: A Million Pennies

Henry was born in Lincoln, in 1899, to David (a chimney sweep) and Jane Tyler. He was one of 10 children, and the family were raised in a terraced house at 5, Bridge Street, Lincoln. His first job, after leaving school, was at Blankney Hall where he worked as a groom.

He married Margaret Hardy in her home town of Gateshead in 1923, and the couple then rented a house at 11, Lonsdale Place (off Thesiger Street), Lincoln. Their first baby was born later the same year, and they would go on to have five more children. Henry joined the British Army at some time in the 1930s and served for 12 years. By the end of the war, the family had moved to 5, Lucy Tower Street, Lincoln, and Henry started earning a modest living by selling costume jewellery and trinkets from a market stall at the corner of Sincil Street and Cornhill.

At some point in 1946, Henry acquired a white Sealyham Terrier which he intended to sell from his market stall. People would stop and stroke the adorable puppy but after several weeks had passed, the dog remained unsold and Henry had grown rather fond of it himself. He gave it the name "Snips". Henry then had the idea of raising money for good causes by charging people a penny to stroke the dog. Snips was extremely popular, and the pennies started to pile up. Henry opened a savings account in Snips' name and the amount recorded in his green bank book grew rapidly.

In 1953, a heavy storm-surge flooded vast areas of the Lincolnshire coast resulting in devastating damage and the loss of 53 lives. Henry donated over £1,000 to the relief fund in the name of Snips. Similarly, he donated £500 to the Hungarian Relief Fund to help refugees after the revolution in that country in 1956. Henry also cared about the people in his own city, by collecting for the County Hospital, and by organising tea parties and concerts for old aged pensioners.

By 1961, Snips was 15 years old, and he passed away peacefully in his sleep, having raised almost £5,000 for good causes. A local newspaper calculated that the sum represented over 1 million pennies (see footnote).

What happened next?

Henry gave up his market stall shortly after Snips died and became a park keeper in the city. However, there was still a healthy balance in the green book and Henry continued to hold regular events for pensioners until he passed away unexpectedly at the age of 66 in 1966.

In April 1967, his widow Margaret, presented a cheque for £712 to the Lincoln Association for the Care of the Elderly as a final act of charity from Snips' bank account.

On Friday July 21st, 1995, Henry's son Phillip unveiled a bronze plaque commemorating Snips on the Corn Exchange building, close to where Henry had his stall. Sadly, the plaque was removed in 2017 as part of the Cornhill Quarter redevelopment project, and its current whereabouts is unknown.

Primary sources:
Lincolnshire Echo, March 5th, 1954
Lincolnshire Echo, July 11th, 1995

Footnote:

Prior to the introduction of decimal currency in the United Kingdom in 1971, there were 12 pennies to a shilling, and 20 shillings to a pound (240 pennies in total).

70: Doris Ashby

Lincoln - 1947: Husband had Secrets!

Doris Elizabeth Emily Ashby was born in Lincoln on November 6th, 1917. She was the only child of Charles (a railway guard) and Maria Ashby of 6, Yarborough Terrace, Lincoln. After leaving school she worked as a shop assistant in the electrical department of a store in the city centre. She managed to resist the temptation of gallant airmen who were stationed in the Lincoln area during World War 2 but, in February, 1947, Doris (then aged 29) met a dashing army officer who was stationed at nearby Canwick.

George Alfred Drury, originally from Yorkshire, was a major in the Pioneer Corps who had served with distinction in India during the war. He looked younger than his 45 years, and made no secret of the fact he was a divorced man. After a whirlwind courtship, the couple got married on April 7th, 1947, and then lived with Doris' parents, who had recently moved to 66, Dixon Street, Lincoln. George resigned his commission, and obtained work in a local engineering works as a turret operator (see footnote).

Life was good for Doris until she answered a knock at the door on Saturday, September 27th, 1947. The woman said, "Good afternoon. I am Ida. I am George's wife." After regaining her composure, Doris invited the woman into the house and learned that George had married Ida in 1930 and they had two sons aged 16 and 12. They had not lived together for several years, but were still legally married. Doris also discovered that George was supposed to be paying towards the upkeep of his two boys, but Ida had not received a penny from him since George was posted overseas in 1941.

Over the following weeks, Ida attempted to claim what she was rightly owed but, after numerous excuses from George, she lost her patience and made a formal complaint of bigamy against him. George was taken into custody and appeared before Lincoln Magistrates on Saturday, December 13th, 1947. Doris sat at the back of the court and followed the court proceedings carefully. Then, just when she thought things could not get any worse, she learned that George was a serial bigamist.

Not only had George married Ida Green in 1930, but he had married for a second time whilst he was in India. Faith Helena Butland was the daughter of a marine engineer from Devon and had gone out to India to act as a nursing sister in the Punjab. The couple were married on February 1st, 1944, in the residence of the Governor of Bengal, and returned to Plympton, Devon, in 1945. They then had a child of their own in February, 1946, before George was posted to Lincolnshire.

George was released on bail in his own recognisance, and appeared before Mr Justice Cassels on February 9th, 1948. He pleaded Guilty. Before sentence was passed, Doris took to the stand and said, "I forgive him for everything he has done because he has been so good to me, and I am only waiting for the day when we can be legally married". The Judge sentenced George to three years penal servitude and observed, "I wonder if she will be of the same opinion after she has waited for a while?"

What happened next?

Ida divorced George whilst he was in prison, and raised the two boys on her own. She passed away in Pontefract in 1976, aged 75.

Faith's marriage to George was annulled after his conviction for bigamy. She subsequently married a man named Edward Burdock in 1953, and the couple had a daughter of their own in 1957. Faith died in Plymouth in 1976 aged 58.

Doris waited for George to be released from prison. Doris and George then went through a legal marriage ceremony in 1950, and had a daughter of their own in 1951. The couple were still living at 66 Dixon Street, when George passed away in 1964, aged 62. Doris never remarried and went on to have a very long life as a widow. She passed away in Lincoln in 2012, aged 95.

Primary source: Lincolnshire Echo, February 9th, 1948

Footnotes:

A turret operator produced precision parts from metal using advanced milling machines.

Three of the children, who were fathered by George in his various relationships, are thought to be still alive. The author has chosen to respect their privacy.

71: Beryl Collingham

Lincoln - 1948: "If I don't jump..."

Beryl Irene Constance Collingham was born in Lincoln on April 14th, 1919, to Herbert (a pattern maker) and Alice Collingham. The family lived at 31, Abbott Street, Lincoln, and Beryl was one of five children. Her father was a hard-working man, but suffered from depression. The 1939 Register shows that he was a patient at the mental hospital at Bracebridge Heath.

After leaving school, Beryl trained as a tracer and gained employment at a nearby engineering firm where she was subsequently involved in the production of munitions during World War 2. After the war she re-trained as a stenographer.

At 11:45am on Monday, October 25th, 1948, Beryl told her mother that she was going shopping. Later that afternoon she went to Lincoln Cathedral and spent some time wandering around inside, before making her way to the foot of the central tower. She seemed to be in good spirits and joked with the attendant as she paid the 1 shilling admission fee. She then climbed 338 steps up the tower and emerged onto a small flat roof. Moments later, she had climbed some 7 feet up one of the pinnacles and stood on a narrow ledge. It is thought that Beryl was on the ledge for over an hour before two women saw her from the street below. They rushed into the cathedral and informed officials of what they had seen.

Constable Edward Ford was the first police officer to arrive. He noticed that Beryl's face was blue with cold and that she was shivering uncontrollably. The officer asked, "What are you doing out there lass?" Beryl replied, "I'm going to jump in a minute." Constable Ford said, "No, don't do that; come here and tell me your troubles, and we can put things right." Beryl responded by saying, "You can't put this right - no one can put this right. The trouble was there when I woke up this morning. I am going to jump."

The officer continued trying to calmly negotiate with her until 5:30pm, by which time it was starting to get dark, and a large crowd had gathered in the road below. Beryl then took one last look at her native city and said, "If I don't jump, these people will be disappointed!" She then launched herself from the pinnacle and plunged to the ground some 240 feet below. Beryl landed on a patch of grass and was killed instantly.

A Coroner's Inquest was held on Thursday, October 28th, and heard evidence from Constable Ford, and staff from the cathedral, about the events leading up to her death. The Coroner then heard from Doctor Crisp who said that Beryl had previously complained about constant pains in her eyes, nose and throat. He had referred her to a specialist but the cause of her pain remained a mystery. He concluded by saying that Beryl had been placed under a lot of strain at work recently and that this had been worrying her. The Coroner recorded a verdict of, "Suicide while of unsound mind."

Beryl was 29 years old and had never married. She was buried in plot J43 at St Swithin's Cemetery on October 29th, 1948.

Primary source: Nottinghamshire Journal, October 29th, 1948

72: Ruth & Horace Evans
Lincoln - 1949: An Air-Crash Fireball

Ruth was born at Worksop in 1911 to Samuel (a coal miner) and Emma Thompson. She was the eldest of six children and, during her childhood, the family lived at 119 Newgate, Worksop. After leaving school, she trained to be a typist and worked for the Inland Revenue at Birkenhead (Merseyside).

It is not known where she met Horace Evans. He was originally from Nottingham, but the 1939 Register shows he was living in Worcester and was employed as a wholesale trader specialising in weighing and testing machines. When World War 2 was declared, he joined the RAF as an officer. The couple married in Nottingham during the summer of 1941, and their first son, Stephen, was born two years later.

The family moved to Lincolnshire after the war, and Horace gained employment as a senior manager for a printing firm in Lincoln. Their second child, Roger, was born at Cherry Willingham in 1947. Then, 18 months later, they moved to 46, Hawthorn Road, Lincoln.

In August 1949, the family decided to take a short break to visit Ruth's relatives who lived near Belfast. They had a pleasant flight from Ringway Airport, Manchester, and the weather was kind to them during their stay. Their return flight was on a 28-seat Dakota DC3 aeroplane operated by British European Airways from Nutts Corner Airport, near Crumlin. Captain Pinkerton requested an extra 100 gallons of fuel for the flight as he expected to encounter some cloud once he was over England. The plane took off with a crew of three and 29 passengers (see footnote) at 11:45am, on Friday, August 18th. The flight was completely uneventful but, shortly after passing over the English coast near Southport, the Dakota entered dense cloud.

Vincent Taylor was a 15-year-old Boy Scout from Oldham who was hiking on Saddleworth Moor, some 15 miles to the east of Manchester. Shortly after 1pm, he heard the sound of a very low-flying aeroplane and looked up. He caught a glimpse of the Dakota, with its undercarriage down. It turned towards the hillside then, seconds later, he heard a crash followed by an explosion. Vincent quickly made his way down to the village of Greenfield and raised the alarm.

A group of a dozen men from the village made their way up the mountain, over very difficult terrain, to a deep gulley where the Dakota had crashed. Wreckage was strewn across a wide area, and was burning fiercely. Jack Smallman was the first to arrive, and he soon came across Horace Evans who was lying injured on the ground about 50 yards from the burning fuselage. He refused to accept any help, and insisted the men should go and search for his wife and children. Arthur Sykes and Ronald Kilshaw subsequently found Ruth some distance from the aircraft. She was very badly burned and was cradling five-year-old Stephen in her arms. Over the next few hours, medical staff and other rescuers arrived on the scene. Eight survivors were carried down the mountain on stretchers and taken to Oldham Infirmary. Sadly, 21 passengers and all three crew members perished in the blaze.

Ruth Evans was badly burned about her arms and face, and remained in hospital for several weeks. Horace was detained for two weeks with a broken leg and minor head injuries. Five-year-old Stephen had minor burns, and was discharged the following day into the care of his uncle, Alan Evans, from Wallington. Tragically, Stephen's younger brother, Roger, was not amongst the survivors.

A Coroner's Inquest was held in Saddleworth on September 29th, 1949. Evidence was given that the aircraft had a certificate of air safety and had been maintained meticulously. However, the aircraft's marker beacon receiver had been replaced the day before the fatal flight and had received further attention shortly before take-off. The Jury heard that, if this device was still malfunctioning, then this could account for why the aircraft was miles away from where it should have been. The Jury returned a verdict of "Death by Misadventure," for each of the victims.

What happened next?

Roger Evans, aged 20 months, was buried at Redhill Cemetery, Arnold, Nottinghamshire on August 24th, 1949.

The Evans family continued to live in Lincoln until Horace retired, and then moved to Poole in Dorset. Ruth passed away in 1992 aged 81, and Horace died two years later aged 84.

It is thought that Stephen, who would now be aged 79, is still alive. The author has chosen to respect his privacy

Primary source: Lincolnshire Echo, August 20th, 1949

Footnotes:

From the 1930s until the 1950s, marker beacons were used extensively along airways to provide aircraft with an indication of their position. They are now gradually being deactivated as RNAV navigation and GPS instruments have made marker beacons obsolete.

As there were 29 passengers on an aircraft which seated 28 people, it is presumed that baby Roger was sitting on Ruth's knee for the flight.

Biography

The author was born in Lancashire in the 1950s but has lived in Lincolnshire for over fifty years.

He joined Lincolnshire Police after leaving school in 1976 and served at Sleaford, Spalding, Skegness, Grantham, Lincoln, Saxilby, Gainsborough and North Hykeham. During his service he studied part-time and obtained a BSc *(hons)* in Psychology and a Post Graduate Certificate in Criminology. He specialised in the field of Crime Reduction and was elected as a Fellow of the Security Institute. Mick retired with the rank of sergeant after thirty years of service.

Mick met his wife Sue whilst serving in Grantham and they married in 1979. They have four grown-up children and ten grandchildren.

Other titles by the same author

Lincoln True Tales from History
ISBN: 9798514019168
Amazon (2021) – Paperback or Kindle

Lincolnshire True Tales from History
ISBN: 9798410598170
Amazon (2021) – Paperback or Kindle

Lincolnshire Women Who Kill (1722 – 2022)
ISBN: 9798352319683
Amazon (2022) – Paperback or Kindle

Printed in Dunstable, United Kingdom